MAYNARD
Massachusetts

MAYNARD
Massachusetts
A House in the Village

JAN VOOGD

Charleston London

History
PRESS

Published by The History Press
Charleston, SC 29403
www.historypress.net

Cover image: "Sunny Afternoon." *Marci Cohen.*

First published 2007

Manufactured in the United Kingdom

ISBN 978.1.59629.205.5

Library of Congress Cataloging-in-Publication Data

Voogd, Jan.
  Maynard, Massachusetts : a house in the village / Jan Voogd.
     p. cm.
  Includes bibliographical references.
  ISBN 978-1-59629-205-5 (alk. paper)
1. Maynard (Mass.)--History--19th century--Anecdotes. 2. Maynard (Mass.)--History--20th century--Anecdotes. 3. Maynard (Mass.)--Social conditions--Anecdotes. 4. Social problems--Massachusetts--Maynard--History--Anecdotes. 5. City and town life--Massachusetts--Maynard--History--Anecdotes. 6. Maynard (Mass.)--Biography--Anecdotes. I. Title.
  F74.M46V66 2007
  974.4'4--dc22
                              2007003571.

To Mac,

for now

CONTENTS

Contents

PREFACE

This work is an example of what I call a "place memoir," which is a selective history that captures the unique spirit of a particular location. A place memoir is not comprehensive, nor does it try to be; rather it relates the telling anecdote here, explores the intriguing mystery there and knits scattered pieces of history together—making connections, placing the pieces in a broader context, finding significance and meaning in what might otherwise be a dry list of names or dates.

Writing about the past can be challenging, both practically and theoretically. On the practical side, for example, Maynard's old newspapers exist only on one set of microfilm, kept safely in the new and beautiful public library that has limited hours of access. In the theoretical realm, history holds many stories that show the dark side of people and places, and while these are often the stories that have the most to teach us, the telling of them can bring unintended impact or unwanted attention to particular individuals. In such cases we are forced to measure wherein lies the greater good—the telling of the story, or the protection of silence.

Thanks to the Maynard Town Archives for the use of many images. Additional thanks goes to Peg Brown, member of the Maynard Historical Commission and board member of the Maynard Historical Society, for the use of many other images, her editing of the photos and for all the information and advice she provided.

Thanks to Janet Young and Cassandra Oxley for comments, erudition and inspiration, and to Sharlene Voogd Cochrane—sister, scholar, sensei. Finally, thanks to Marci and Java Cohen, for finding present-day Maynard and reminding me to get out and enjoy it.

A caveat to the reader: As much as we might like to think otherwise, history is simply not permanent. The truth itself doesn't change, what actually happened doesn't change, but history is only how we comprehend the past. History lives, subject to our understanding of it and our representation of it, waiting only for someone to come forward with more information or a new interpretation. The stories told here come from what I could discover, up until the moment that I am writing. With this, I offer you the spirit of Maynard, Massachusetts, as I have found it, in these, the early days of 2007.

INTRODUCTION

$\mathcal{W}$e have an expression in Maynard. Whether an individual has recently moved to Maynard or has generations of family here, at some point everyone will find the words "only in Maynard" rolling off their tongues. They might not be able to articulate exactly what the words mean, but the saying will absolutely fit the moment at hand. The phrase "only in Maynard" is ultimately responsible for the creation of this book.

Maynard is a unique town in eastern Massachusetts. We are only five square miles. The Assabet River National Wildlife Refuge encompasses almost two of these. The renovated woolen mill complex located downtown is as sprawling as the Prudential Center in Boston is tall. We are therefore ten thousand people living in three square miles. Maynard's dense neighborhoods are carved out by the meandering Assabet River and the historic mill. Maynard is not affluent like its suburban neighbors nor is it agricultural like the apple-growing communities to our west. Maynard functions much like a self-sufficient city but is too small and intimate for that label.

We have a vibrant and eclectic downtown to which most residents can walk. We have a movie theater, a performing arts theater, great restaurants, used everything shops and no grocery store. A quarter of us are retired and a quarter is raising school-aged children. As a small community with many services, we have financial challenges. Also, as a community in which several families have lived for generations, many of us are related. (One must be careful with disparaging remarks; the town employee or committee member of whom you speak could very likely be related to your listener!) We have challenges and we have great pride; therein lays the essence of the expression "only in Maynard."

INTRODUCTION

Last year, our local paper, the *Beacon-Villager*, began a feature called "Only in Maynard." I helped to recruit a revolving cadre of six local contributors for the column. The idea was to give diverse folks an opportunity to explore what "only in Maynard" meant to them. One contributor wrote about his close-knit neighborhood. One wrote about the warm reception she and her partner received as an urban transplant lesbian couple. The column was very well received.

A few of the "Only in Maynard" columnists chose to focus on Maynard history. Jan Voogd was one of them. This book is a result of the research and unique perspective Jan brought to her column every six weeks or so. The setting for Jan's research may be Maynard, but each chapter also transcends place. This collection features some colorful and controversial episodes. While the specifics are peculiar to Maynard, the broader issues are national. Each chapter reflects the growing pains of an evolving nation. Whether the reader ever steps foot in Maynard, Massachusetts, *A House in the Village* sheds light on common issues of immigration, the Industrial Revolution and political expression. Hopefully, readers will finish this collection with a more complex understanding of these issues as experienced in one small town.

In *The People's History of the United States*, Howard Zinn challenged us with other perspectives on our national stories. Similarly, the chapters before you may stir up feelings and stimulate thinking. History may record the facts, but there is always more than one interpretation. Jan Voogd's intriguing collection is thoroughly researched and makes for great reading. It offers one interpretation on one small town's history.

Sally Bubier
Chairman of the Board of Selectmen

Chapter 1

A House in the Village
The Village Colonial

The sun rises behind the big red brick mill, setting alight the heart of the village: the mill pond. Encircling the pond are the full range of homes represented in Maynard, from the typical "village colonials" to subsidized multifamily dwellings to a stately and rambling mill-owner domicile. All are equal around this pond now, all share in the rich pageant of Maynard life, all offer their own version of prosperity or pathos.

The mill pond itself holds within it the range of Maynard's contrasts or contradictions. Arguably the most beautiful setting in town, the pond smoothly reflects the pattern of factory bricks, the sunrises, the sunsets and the moonlight. At the same time, it is bordered by a stretch of the most uninspired architecture, the addresses that appear most frequently in the town police report. The mill pond has been the scene of many a happy occasion, with people fishing and canoeing, and its shore hosting the popular Farmers' Market on summer Saturdays. Yet, it has also been the scene of sadness, as on Christmas Day in 1928, when the Minko cousins, eight and ten, fell through the ice and drowned.

Like Manhattan, part of Maynard, which at the time was part of Sudbury, was purchased from the area aboriginals. William Gutteridge notes that in 1684 "Edmund Goodenow and others" paid sixty dollars to "Jehojakim and twelve other Indians" for the land. This was after things had settled down from the excitement of King Philip's War in 1676, when "probably all or nearly all [the] white settlers of this section [were] wiped out." The Indians waging the attacks were believed to have been from some place distant, as the local Nobscot people were considered friendly.

At the mill and the pond beats the heart of the town. *Peg Brown*.

While Maynard was settled by the English and Scottish and joined by the Irish after the 1847 potato famine, many other peoples have followed. The Maynard Historical Commission established that in the 1880s the "Russo-Finns" came to town, and by the 1920s they were a quarter to a third of the population. From 1899 on, there were Poles, Lithuanians, Russian, Italians, Swedes, Norwegians and Danes. In more recent years, they have been joined by Brazilians and people from India. The various immigrant groups influenced the housing styles in town.

Just as New Orleans has its shotgun house, "one room wide and several rooms deep, their narrow facades defined by a modest front porch," as Robin Langley Sommer defines it; just as Santa Fe has its adobe cottages with Spanish tile roofs; as Boston's Back Bay has its brownstone town houses; and as Dorchester its three-family triple-deckers, so too does Maynard have its village colonials. A simple, intrepid little wood-frame cottage, built for the mill workers, the village colonial is found all over town and is a stunning example of true vernacular architecture. While detailing such as stone tracery was often done in wood to save expense, the spare, plain houses of Maynard forfeited even that. Yet today every village colonial in Maynard has its own distinctive appearance, due to the individualized alterations made by the folks living within, often accomplished by their own untrained handiwork. Though originally all identical, no longer are any two of these houses the same. While most are expanded by an additional room or two, some have extensive multifloor supplements. Some have been altered in

14

their façade as well, with elaborate embellishments. There is even a village colonial that has become what appears to be a ski chalet, across from the corner store on Parker Street. The term village colonial is an example of what Noam Chomsky has called "transformational grammar." Real estate agents in the area have for years been calling the ubiquitous two-level cottage by the term, but it is occasionally used to describe other house styles.

The English Colonial is a symmetrical rectangular façade of 1½ to 2 stories with a peaked roof. The English Colonial cottage is same shape but smaller. Maynard's Village Colonial is the English Colonial cottage, but turned on its side. There is sometimes an attic vent in the third (or 2½) story, sometimes not. The turn allows for narrower lots. There is minimal architectural adornment, if any. There may in some cases be a gabled roof, the "triangular portion of an end wall below a ridged roof," as Sommers defines it, or a hipped roof, "the external angle is formed by the meeting of two adjacent sloping sides." The Village Colonial found in Maynard is one of the simplest variations on the English Cottage style, popularized by several pattern books available at the time: A.J. Davis, *Rural Residences*, 1837; Gervase Wheeler, *Rural Homes*, 1851; Calvert Vaux, *Villas and Cottages*, 1857.

Built during the Victorian era (1830s–early 1900s), the mill companies that constructed these houses were not influenced by the many fads and fashions of that period and deliberately chose a modest simplicity. Given that they were building simple homes in the context of a time in which the fashion was just the opposite, what does that say about those who would live in these houses? Perhaps their design, under the influence of the Finnish immigrants, presaged the simplicity of the early modernist movement of Eliel Saarinen or Alvar Aalto, world-renowned Finnish architects. Their work was distinctive for its spare, uncluttered lines, and the village colonial in its basic form was nothing if not that. More likely is that Finns simply felt at home in these plain houses, because while the village colonial is found throughout Maynard, it is not unique to this Finnish-influenced town. In fact, the simple house style was often built in other mill villages in the northeastern United States.

"Teardowns," the specter haunting historical preservationists, in which people buy property for the lot itself, tear down the existing house, and build a McMansion, have come to Maynard. Before too many of the old small houses are gone, we should take note. Maynard citizens can appreciate the fact that the town is one of the picturesque center villages of New England, and one of the few mill villages that have survived the passing of the years and the rising and falling fortunes of the mill intact. In many New England villages today, as Gary Kulik has pointed out, "little more than a ruined dam and parts of mill foundations remain as evidence that [a mill] was ever part of the landscape…Village mills and tenements that remain are usually incorporated into towns that look unrecognizably different from their early nineteenth-century form—often overrun by suburbs." Maynard has avoided this fate so far, but is now in danger of developers who ignore the charm and history of the town's small houses.

Despite its history, Maynard as yet has no official historic districts, which means anyone can do anything to a historic house—and they have. *Old House Journal* calls it "re-muddling." Historic houses in Maynard are not about what Marjorie Garber calls the "insufferable pretension" or the "Laura Ashley and Merchant-Ivory" restoration of a "sanitized historic sensibility that falsifies, and prettifies, the grittier facts of the past." Instead, the renovations are the reclaiming of a humble solidity, an almost Shaker plainness.

As Garber has pointed out, "one of the commodities most prized by American house purchasers is a little piece of history to call their own." She quotes the editor-in-chief of *Country Home* as saying, "There is a finite number of old houses out there…Everyone wants one, but most people can't have them." Maynard has a surprising number of houses built in the 1800s and early 1900s. The miracle of Maynard is that, because of the mill, there are many old houses here, and they are not the typical old house—big, Victorian or a rambling old farmhouse. Instead the small and cottage-like village colonial is perfect for singles, or for couples without children, who because of age or gender or profession are at the lower end of the purchasing power grid. This reasonably priced historic housing stock, amply supplied in Maynard, enabled my partner and me to acquire our own little piece of history.

A House in the Village

Above: This village colonial today still has only the most simple of additions. *Eve Berman.*

Opposite: The haphazard charm of Maynard's houses peeks out of this bird's-eye view. *Peg Brown.*

Our village colonial was standing at the time of the first assessment in 1871, when Maynard became a town, and some information suggests that one of the early owners was a town constable. The house apparently was added onto twice—gaining first a kitchen and bath at some point, then a porch in the 1940s, which was later made into a regular room. The crawl space under the porch took in castoff material over the years, and has offered up bygone newspapers, clothing and mysterious bones. Coming from a tiny urban apartment in nearby Somerville, this Maynard house, at least 130 years old, offered unparalleled space, a driveway, a yard and even a shed, for the price. Buying it was a forgone conclusion. Little did we know that in acquiring this house, we were getting a town—and what a town, indeed.

Much more elaborate additions and enhancements adorn this village colonial. *Eve Berman*.

Chapter 2

FINNISH BATHS MURDER MYSTERY
Ethnic Traditions Corrupted

*O*nce settled into the house, I began to wonder what all had happened in the 130 years this home had stood. One of the first Saturday afternoons in the yard of the new house, a neighbor from up the street and I were chatting.

"You know," she said, conspiratorially, "George W. Bush and his family went to a backyard barbeque at your next-door neighbor's once."

"Really?"

"Yes. There were secret service cars all up and down the street!"

"You're kidding."

"No. Well, maybe they weren't secret service. It was before he was president. It was when he was governor of Texas. Well, maybe it was before he was governor. But it was definitely George W. No doubt about that."

With this warning beacon of rumor as my watchword, I set out to learn what I could about the stories in Maynard's past. In my line of work as a librarian, with many databases easily accessible to me, I started with a full-text legal resource, searching the name of the street and the name of the town within Massachusetts state case law, just to see what it might tell me about what had officially transpired in the neighborhood. Nothing came up for my house, but because the name of the street is also the name of a type of tree, my journey into the history of Maynard was launched. It seems one night in 1940, a car crashed into a tree alongside Route 117, a man died, and the circumstances surrounding the incident remain veiled by time.

The story begins with the Finnish bath, or sauna, which was an integral part of daily life in Finland. When Finns immigrated to North America, one of the first things they did to make themselves feel more at home was to build a sauna. Normally, each house had its own sauna, but when space was in short supply in towns or urban areas, they would build a public Finnish bath. Between 1850 and 1920, about 400,000 people left Finland to settle in this country and Canada. Most settled in Michigan, Minnesota and Wisconsin, but a significant number came to Maynard and became mill workers. Over the years, they built five public Finnish baths on Powder Mill Road, Florida Street and River Bank Road. In 1971 Maynard's Historical Commission noted that two saunas were still operating, one as a "private club" (built on River Street in 1903), the other on Elmwood Street.

For Finns, the baths were nearly as sacred as church. An expression of Finnish identity, the saunas provided sanctuary and restored health. Often a log cabin, each sauna had an oven in one corner made of boulders, where a wood fire burned until the rocks were intensely hot. The sauna's inhabitants threw buckets of cold water on the rocks, creating clouds of hot steam. One small window provided light and ventilation.

This posed shot offers a glimpse of some of the town's storied inhabitants. *Maynard Town Archives.*

Melissa Ladenheim described the sauna experience as a three-stage process: first perspiration, then washing, then cooling off, and it could be repeated many times. On the traditional Friday or Saturday night sauna, families and neighbors came together as a group to reaffirm their common cultural identity. Once in the sauna, the new, strange, non-Finnish world was left behind. Afterward coffee and pulla bread rounded out the ritual.

A vernacular Maynard-area Finnish sauna. *Maynard Town Archives.*

There is little evidence of how the non-Finns in Maynard felt about the saunas, but farmers in Minnesota with many Finnish neighbors were puzzled and complained to authorities. "What is this strange nocturnal rite?" they wondered. In his field research published in 1963, Cotton Mather found that they thought the Finns were "worshipping pagan gods in strange log temples—seen from time to time cavorting naked in the moonlight in what seemed to be ritualistic dances."

In Minnesota in 1880, a sauna actually went on trial. Yvonne R. Lockwood tells of a non-Finn farmer who went to court to

> rid the countryside of "that pagan temple." On the day of the trial, the courtroom was packed with curious citizens, most of whom never heard of a sauna. But it was proved to the judge's satisfaction that the Finns were law abiding, American citizens of a staid Lutheran caliber when it was explained the sauna was a place for cleaning and not for worshipping pagan gods. The judge ordered the plaintiff to pay the defendant thirty dollars for damages to his reputation plus forty dollars to have the sauna moved to a more isolated location.

Mather attributed the problem in part to communication. The language barrier made it difficult to explain the role the sauna played in Finnish culture. There is no English equivalent to explain such sauna-related words as *vihta*, *kinas* and *loyly*. The practice of entire groups bathing together, regardless of age or gender, could be easily misconstrued as being immodest or immoral or worse.

This country is a melting pot, however, and saunas have meant different things to other cultures. Once non-Finns got past their initial reservations, they often adopted the Finnish baths as their own. To the dismay of their Finnish builders, the baths were sometimes then turned into brothels and places for other illicit activity. "A Turkish bath is not a sauna," Mikel Aaland heard from the Finnish spokespeople over and over again. "Nor is the sauna a place to hide illicit sex." More than any other misunderstandings, Finns were outraged that American saunas were being used as brothels. Ladenheim found a striking example of how the sauna has now been co-opted. A Finnish American woman reported her American-born children asking, "What do you call the sauna in Finnish?" Of course, the Finnish word for it is "sauna," pronounced quickly, but as if it were three syllables—sawuna.

Despite the controversy, or perhaps because of it, the bathhouse phenomenon was accepted in New England, and men came from miles around to visit the baths in Maynard. This is why there was a fateful crossing of paths on a late summer night. Maynard locals insist that, while non-Finns had begun frequenting the baths, nothing unwholesome went on. From the details of the court case, though, it would seem that for some, taking a sauna was complemented by drinking.

One such out-of-towner with his own reasons for visiting the baths was an artist from Wellesley. Ultimately, he found himself charged with murder. Another out-of-towner was a young man of twenty-one, whose path led from Arlington to the baths at Maynard and, finally, to his death by the side of Route 117. When in the newspaper I first related this story, whose particulars are a matter of public record, members of the family expressed distress at seeing the story printed. This situation illustrates the constant tension between knowing the truth and fearing it. Lev Goriansky wrote at least two books, one about the Hagia Sofia and the other about the fine arts in higher education. In both he stresses the importance of the search for truth.

Goriansky graduated from college in Russia and then served in the navy for seven years, including during the First World War. Later he studied art and architecture in the United States and worked for various widely recognized architectural firms, most in New York. He became disillusioned with architecture and the time commitment it required. He felt that giving up all of one's free time would stifle the creative spirit of a mystically inclined person, such as he was. Perhaps if he had not had so much free time in the evenings, what happened that night could have been avoided.

Maple & Brook Sts.,
Maynard, Mass.

A fork in the road offers alternate routes. Could John F. Sheehan's sad fate have been avoided by taking a different path? *Peg Brown.*

According to the trial testimony, and all the quotes are from those documents, on August 23, 1940, shortly before 10:00 p.m., Goriansky drove his wife's 1936 coupe from his home in Wellesley to Maynard, where he spent about an hour and a half in a Finnish bath on Florida Street and two "cafés," or taverns. Afterward, between 11:30 and midnight, ready to return to Wellesley, he discovered that his car wouldn't start. No garage was open, and the car was parked in the street near a light, so he began working on the engine himself. As he was doing so, a drunken man appeared behind him, at first talking to himself, then asking for a cup of coffee.

Goriansky did not stop his work on the engine, but gave the man two nickels without turning around, and said, "Go away, don't bother me." Eventually, Goriansky got the car running and drove to another café just up the road. When he returned to his car from this café and got in, the man to whom Goriansky had given the coins appeared in the passenger window, "worn out and drunk," and asked him for "a lift."

When he saw the drunken man, Goriansky testified, he closed the window and locked the door. Perhaps Goriansky remembered it that way, but an automobile dealer testified later in the trial that this model of automobile could only be locked with a key from the outside. The man was four or five inches above the line of the top of the glass, which was about at his eyebrows. As he stood leaning over, his forehead was close to the window, against it. Goriansky did not know where the man's feet were, because he could not see his legs. The stranger gripped the handle and jiggled it. Goriansky started his car "with a big jerk." The stranger was swearing, and the nervous artist drove off, "full speed towards home."

"Why were you nervous?" came the question from the court.

Goriansky said, "He annoyed me. I thought he wanted to hold me up or something."

At that point it was about midnight, and Goriansky took Route 117 toward Waltham. The stranger would supposedly have been standing on the running board, clinging to the handle. There were no other cars on the road, until about two or three miles outside of Maynard, when Goriansky claims he was blinded by the headlights of another automobile, approaching on the wrong side of the road. Goriansky was moving at thirty-five or forty miles an hour, and in swerving to avoid the oncoming car, part of his car went onto the dirt shoulder. Apparently losing control of the car, he increased speed and ran head-on into a telegraph pole located in the underbrush. The right side of the bumper split and snapped off the pole, which remained wedged between the right front fender and the bumper. A crack traversed the driver's side of the windshield and the headlight on the right side was shattered, but there was no visible damage to the running board.

Goriansky went to a nearby house and told the woman there that he'd had a bad accident. At that time he said, "There is a man hurt very badly," but when he was later taken to a hospital by some young men in an automobile, he told them that he had been alone. Later, Goriansky told a state police officer that at the time of the accident he thought someone was trying to kill him and he had a fear of impending death.

Between 10:30 and 11:00 a.m. the next morning, the body of a man was found in thick shrubbery off the road near the trunk of a pine tree. He was identified as John F. Sheehan Jr., who had just before midnight left a Finnish bath on Powder Mill Road in the company of three other young men. He was found to have a blood alcohol level equivalent to "about three shots of whiskey." The pine tree stood sixteen feet beyond the telegraph pole. Less than a foot up from the ground the bark of the tree was freshly scraped off in "an irregular scar four inches long and two and a half to three inches wide. There was blood on the ground near the body."

In the area near the tree were parts of the automobile and pieces of broken glass from the headlight. According to the medical examiner, death had occurred between 10:00 p.m. and 4:00 a.m., caused by a skull fracture, "due to being thrown violently against a fixed object. The scar in the trunk contained hairs from the deceased's head. Bark from the tree was found in the head and trouser legs. On the palms of the hands and on the fingers there was grease like that from an automobile."

A bloodstained suede glove belonging to Goriansky's wife lay on Sheehan's chest, near his necktie. The matching glove was on the shelf in the back of the car. "The coupe had only one seat inside, and that was for the driver. Beside the driver there was a 'baby seat,' and a passenger would have to ride in the rumble seat. Following the accident the rumble seat was found closed. The spare tire mounted on the rear was 'off to one side,' and its metal cover was off. The right hand door was locked."

Lev Goriansky admitted that the circumstantial evidence suggested that Sheehan was killed when Goriansky's car collided with the pole. All those present agreed that it was reasonable to think Sheehan had been somewhere on the car, because he had automobile grease on his hands even though he had just been at the baths. Because there were no broken bones or other injuries, it was unlikely Sheehan had been struck while walking along the highway. If not riding on or in the car, Sheehan probably could not have gotten to the place his body was found, at least two miles outside of Maynard, in the limited time between his leaving the baths and the moment of the collision. This idea is made stronger by Goriansky's testimony that he saw no other automobile before reaching the scene. Finally, if Sheehan were on the car as a trespasser, as Goriansky suggested, he still had the right to expect that Goriansky would not wantonly or recklessly expose him to danger.

Goriansky continued to insist that he did not know Sheehan was on the automobile. The jury had to decide if Sheehan could have been on the car somehow, without Goriansky being aware of him. Sheehan could have been on the right running board in a crouching posture, gripping the door handle or maintaining a tenuous hold in some other way. It was likely that he was thrown from the right running board into the tree when the speeding car crashed to a complete stop against the pole. Since there was no damage to the rear of the car except for the spare tire being off kilter and without its metal cover, Goriansky's suggestion that Sheehan must have been holding onto the spare tire on the rear is not entirely plausible. Even if he had been hanging on in back, the momentum of the crash would likely have sent Sheehan into the car, rather than throwing him sixteen feet forward.

The judge instructed the jury that they did not have to believe Goriansky when he testified that a photograph of Sheehan was not the man who first asked for coffee money and later for a ride, or that Sheehan was not on the running board. More important was Goriansky's testimony that after the car started with a big jerk, he heard the man swearing. Furthermore, Goriansky would have seen a man the size of Sheehan, five feet ten inches and 175 pounds, on the running board long enough to travel two miles, or at least he would have noticed a sagging of the automobile.

The jury deliberated and found that Goriansky intentionally turned the automobile onto a dirt shoulder and increased speed, in an effort to harm or eject the passenger. When the car ran head-on into the pole, Sheehan was thrown against the tree and killed. The official opinion was that Goriansky meant to brush Sheehan off the running board, but didn't mean to kill him. Sheehan's estate was awarded damages, but Goriansky never paid, and Sheehan's family fought in court for seven years to get the money from the insurance company.

Two years earlier, Goriansky had written in his book *The Fine Arts* that "true art education should endeavor to deal with all faculties of each student, cultivate his senses, and educate him to produce a harmonious and equal unfoldment of his powers, in order that his special aptitudes should find their full natural development." It is especially sad then, because of the events of the night at the baths in Maynard, John Sheehan, at twenty-one years old, would never have that opportunity.

What happened that night, after both men had been at the Finnish baths? Who patronized the baths, and what went on there? Were the baths still truly Finnish, or had others adapted them for their own purposes? Were they, in fact, brothels, or used for some other kind of illicit activity? Was Goriansky telling the whole story about that night? Who was trying to kill whom?

The story of this mysterious tragedy was the beginning of my journey into Maynard's rich history. The elements uncovered here were so wide ranging, and the questions provoked were so various, that it would have been impossible to keep from searching for the layers of meaning to be revealed.

Chapter 3

MILL MANAGER SUGGESTS WORKERS SHOULD STRIKE

What Would the Boss Do?

What other strange stories lurk in Maynard's past? A historical newspaper database provides the searchable full text of several major U.S. newspapers. A simple search on the name of the town, limited first to the *New York Times*, and then expanded to several large newspapers, turned up an extraordinary number of tales. From the odd to the trite to the tragic, these stories described all manner of people—some from Maynard, some in Maynard—and all manner of events.

Being a mill town, many of Maynard's stories, directly and tangentially, begin or end with the mill. One of the stories illustrating the distinctively local approach to things involved a group of workers who refused to go on strike until the company superintendent told them they should.

In 1919 the labor unions were working hard to get employers to cut back to a forty-eight-hour workweek. Most New England mills ran fifty-four-hour weeks, including the Assabet Mill, a unit of the American Woolen Company. Any mill that didn't cut back to forty-eight hours on the third of February would see their workers out on strike. What's more, the unions in several of the American Woolen Company mills in Lawrence, Massachusetts, demanded to keep receiving their fifty-four hours' pay. Unlike the Lawrence unionists, the union members at the Assabet Mill did not demand the extra pay.

Striking was not unprecedented at the Assabet Mill, although it did not happen as often as at other American Woolen Company factories. In January of 1902, the *Atlanta Constitution* reported the spinners went out on strike. The mill was shut down except for the carding and sorting departments, leaving about fifteen hundred employees idle. The entire mill was expected to remain closed until the spinners' grievances were met. At issue was a new procedure for weighing the roping used in the spinning department. When the company changed from beam scales to grain scales, it required the spinners to work harder in order to produce a given amount of yarn. The spinners wanted the deficiency in pay for overtime work to be made up with a raise.

Child workers went on strike at the Assabet Mill in 1905. Twenty boy and girl stitchers, working fifty-eight hours a week for $3.96, demanded a raise to $4.50. Their work stoppage threatened to force a temporary mill closure.

This time around, in April 1919, the management of the Lawrence mills refused to pay their workers for fifty-four hours, so those workers went on strike. Some New York City labor activists, including H.J. Rubenstein and W.H. Derrick, came to Maynard representing the views of the radical Lawrence strikers, trying to motivate the Maynard workers to strike as well. The activists brought with them a Polish striker from Lawrence and a Finnish woman, in an attempt to reach the predominantly Finnish and Polish workers in their native language, but even so the Maynard workers were just not persuaded.

According to the *Maynard Enterprise,* a woman weaver said at the time, "Members of Local Union 771, why do you allow outside agitators to come into your midst and try and rush you into a strike vote?" The newspaper also quoted another worker remarking, "Do they think the people of Maynard are d---- fools?" There was, however, a subgroup of the Maynard Weavers' Union that voted to give $500 to the strikers at Lawrence. Even this small gesture of support was not agreeable to the majority of the union, and the treasurer of the Weavers' Union refused to sign over the money.

A view of the mill from the top of Summer Hill, denied today by the verdant tree growth. *Peg Brown.*

This drama caused significant discord in Maynard's union. About forty of the six hundred union weavers wanted to support the Lawrence strikers. These forty weavers left the organization, but they continued to work at the mill. The tension grew to the point that in October, the Weavers' Union passed a vote refusing to work with anyone who was not a member of their union.

Understanding the background, the character and the culture of the Finns as told by numerous scholars will help in understanding the Finnish stance on labor. Like most immigrants, Finns had come to this country for many reasons. A decree in 1878 had made military service for all males compulsory, which Finns considered bad enough, but then a military service law in 1901 declared that all Finnish conscripts would have to serve anywhere in Russia, or even outside it, if at any time called upon to do so. This struck at the heart of the peace loving Finn, who had recently experienced so much war. The Thirty Years' War, Russo-Turkish War of 1877, the World War and the 1918 Red Rebellion buffeted Finland in rapid succession. Other oppressive Russian policies, like those that left only raw herring and skimmed milk for Finland's working class, added to the appeal of America.

Once in America, the Finns were determined to work hard, and Maynard offered the unique combination of opportunities that appealed to them. Finnish immigrants were inclined to take over abandoned and derelict small farms and get them going again, while at the same time working steadily in a factory. This unusual farm and factory combination was possible in Maynard, as the mill was in the center of a small commercial area, but surrounded by acres of challenging farmland and woods. Maynard's own Frank Aaltonen said the Finns were not intimidated by the rugged New England soil because the soil in Finland was just as poor, and that Finns looked for the most difficult work with the biggest pay. Then, when settled, Finns focused on buying or building their own home, which they would keep perfectly clean. They were seen as a frugal people as well. William Hoglund heard that in the parish of Laihia, the people were so frugal that "25 years after lads caught fish in a brook, women drew water from the brook for fish stew."

Finns had played their part in the labor phenomenon of "progressive displacement," in which new immigrants took the jobs at the bottom tier and earlier arrivals moved up into more desirable jobs. Hoglund characterized the competition between immigrant nationalities in Maynard as having intense rivalries, such that Irishmen reportedly went so far as to spit on Finns in the street. By 1919 the Irish were no longer competing for the same tier of work with the Finns, as they had long moved up or out. By this time, it was the Finns who were moving up, and having paid their dues in Maynard, they were likely not inclined to risk their position.

Finnish scholar John Jokinen has written that the labor organization most enthusiastically embraced by the immigrant Finns was the Industrial Workers of the World (IWW). While the American Federation of Labor (AFL) was for the skilled worker, Finns were mostly unskilled. The IWW believed capitalism was the cause of the problems and that all workers were one, regardless of race, creed or color; Finns, being immigrants, were ineligible to vote. Most of the IWW Finns had split from the Finnish Socialist Federation in 1914. In Michigan, Minnesota and Wisconsin, Finns played significant roles in labor disputes and got a reputation as troublemakers. The Finns were particularly calm in Maynard, which makes the situation all the more interesting. To what this could be attributed remains a mystery—maybe the unionists were far outnumbered by the non-unionist churchgoing Finns, or maybe the working conditions were much better at the Assabet Mill. In Lawrence, there appears to be no mention of Finns working at the American Woolen Company. The immigrant workers there were from Italy, Poland, Syria, Canada, Ireland, Turkey, Russia, Austria, Portugal and some were Jewish. The Finns there may have been counted as Russian, but it's quite possible that there may simply not have been many in Lawrence, as they may have just chosen Maynard to settle instead. Historian Ardis Cameron has noted that the IWW is often put at the heart of the 1912 Lawrence strike, and this is the explanation for the intense militancy and solidarity of the strikers. Whatever it was that motivated the solidarity in Lawrence, it was not present in Maynard. Perhaps the conditions in Maynard were just never as bad as they were in Lawrence.

A few days after the discordant union meeting about the Lawrence strikers, the superintendent of the mill, O.C. Dreshler, met with a committee of the weavers to discuss their vote. Dreshler bought some time by telling the committee that he could not simply discharge non-union weavers without cause, but that as opportunities arose, he would fire any weaver who was not a member of the union. When a week or more went by with no results, the group met again with Dreshler. This time, he suggested that the only way to get rid of the non-union weavers would be for the union weavers to go on strike. By doing that, he would not have enough weavers in the shop, and he would be forced to close the mill down. Acting on his suggestion, the Weavers' Union voted to strike.

When the strike started, Dreshler denied that it was his idea, but he later admitted to a Department of Labor conciliator that he did not want to keep the non-union weavers, because, as he was quoted in DOL files, "they were a bad lot of socialists." Once the weavers had been out on strike for two weeks, the other branches of the textile trade at the mill followed, until ultimately 2,300 people were on strike.

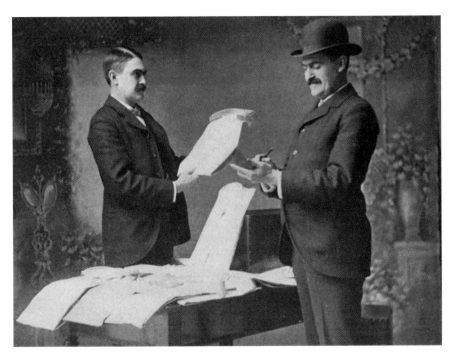

These unknown Maynard businessmen may be mill management or posing as such. *Maynard Town Archives*.

Dreshler was called on the carpet by the company executives for his role in the situation. In a conference with the board of directors of the American Woolen Company, he admitted to telling the weavers he would close down the plant. The chair of the board, William W. Wood, informed Dreshler he had no right or authority to make such a statement, but since the strike had already started, Wood could just as soon fight the battle in Maynard as anywhere else.

William Wood had a loaded history behind him, with his role in the famous Lawrence strike of 1912. Edward G. Roddy characterizes Wood as "the son of poor immigrant parents, born in a small fisherman's cottage." Eventually he became one of America's business and social elite. His American Woolen Company was the largest in the world. Several of the mills that he built were the largest of their kind.

Wood had married the aristocratic Ellen Wheaton Ayer, daughter of Frederick Ayer, owner of Washington Mills, where Wood headed the cotton-manufacturing department. Ellen's brothers had graduated from Harvard, and while Wood never finished high school, he never let this deter him. Wood took charge at the mill and made dramatic changes. As Roddy described it, while "other mill owners predicted disaster…Wood persisted in pressing for increased efficiency, and his father-in-law stood by him."

In 1899 Wood created quite a stir in the woolen manufacturing industry by consolidating eight firms, four from Massachusetts, into one, as the American Woolen Company. From here, Wood acquired, almost obsessively, additional mills year after year. He worked seventeen-hour workdays and had two secretaries and a bank of phones to stay in touch with his widely dispersed staff. A limousine stood by, ready to rush to anywhere in the extensive organization. By 1924 the company workforce numbered 40,000, and it owned sixty mills, of which the mill in Maynard was one. The American Woolen Company built a huge addition to the Assabet Mills.

The Lawrence strike lasted six weeks, and has been called one of the most notable labor conflicts in American industrial history. Riots and other violence among the 30,000 strikers spurred the governor to order in the state militia. The strikers called in the IWW to take charge of the action. The conditions in Lawrence for the workers that they were protesting to change were, in fact, terrible. Wooden three-decker tenement hovels housing three to six hundred people per acre were rife with, as Roddy puts it, "vermin, filthy alleys, voracious rats and evil smells…The mean age at death in Lawrence was a bare fifteen. And by fifteen, many a boy and girl had already been a mill hand" for a year or two.

William Wood may have lost touch with his 25,000 workers. He had been preoccupied with acquisitions, consolidations and expansions. He was a world away from his employees' experience. The foul smells and grime of the tenement district had never reached him. The positive effect of the strike was that he awoke to an understanding of his workers' daily reality.

So, things had gotten better. With the help of his progressively thinking son, who graduated from Harvard in 1915, Wood learned from the mistakes he had made. In February 1919, there was another massive strike in Lawrence for a shorter workweek with no pay cut, and while Wood was the bad guy in 1912, he was not singled out as a target in the 1919 strike because he'd since 1912 given his employees several dramatic pay raises. Bruce Watson reports that just after the 1919 strike, the American Woolen Company gave its workers insurance, maternity leave and sick pay.

Maynard's 1919 labor dispute at the Assabet Mill dragged on, and featured one of the town's first picket lines. Out of a crowd of three thousand striking workers, four hundred formed a line walking back and forth in front of the mill gates. Some of the striking weavers at the heart of the dispute, in distinctive Finnish style, formed a band playing music to accompany the picket line and subsequently to lead the march of two thousand workers through the streets of the downtown. Federal mediators from the U.S.

Department of Labor were called in to help. Unlike the Lawrence strike, where Wood had refused to compromise, quick negotiation soon resolved the strike. The Maynard workers lived in a much better situation than the Lawrence workers had faced. To appease the Weavers' Union, the company management moved the non-union weavers out of the weave-room, down into a room in the cellar. According to the Department of Labor files, the Weavers' Union called off the strike, and 2,300 Maynard workers returned to their jobs.

Chapter 4

EXPLOSIVE HISTORY OF LOCAL MILL
Betrayed by Company Paternalism

Another mill employed many residents of Maynard, and this mill's stories are nearly all dramatic and sad. American Powder Mills, thought of as one of Maynard's "other" mills, operated across the town line in Acton from the late 1800s until W.R. Grace, Inc., bought it in 1954. A main thoroughfare traversing the town takes its name from the powder mill. The work of this mill was particularly dangerous because the "powder" produced was gunpowder. Over the years, many Maynard workers were injured, a few were killed, most of them through no fault of their own. In the worst cases, the accidents left little behind of those killed. The company made many promises to the injured workers and to the survivors of those killed—promises the company ultimately could not, or would not, keep.

The American Cynamid Company General Offices were in Rockefeller Plaza in New York City. The corporation as a whole comprised ten divisions, making products ranging from drugs, sutures and ligatures for the medical field, to chemical fertilizers for agriculture, to the industrial explosives made in the mill in Maynard. The company had sales offices in more than fifty locations throughout the world, including Havana, Cuba; Johannesburg, South Africa; Los Angeles, California; and Maynard. In 1942, because of personnel shortages due to the war, the company began relying on the employment and training of women. Also in 1942, the Department of Justice indicted American Cynamid Company, one of its subsidiaries, one officer and three employees for violations of the antitrust laws. The company settled out of court the next year, for an amount that was at least $453,461. American Cynamid continued to violate antitrust laws, accused on at least two more occasions, once in 1960 and again in 1983. Their name comes up frequently in the files of corporate law.

Explosive History of Local Mill

The mill stored large quantities of gunpowder and dynamite on site, and explosions were frequent. The following entry from the diary of Edward Carver Damon, owner of the Damon Mill in neighboring Concord, gives some idea of the magnitude.

> *Powder Mill blew up at 11:10 and Mr Taylor was so terribly burned that he died before five.* [September 5, 1873] *Dr. Cook called to see me on his way home from the Powder Mills. At 8:10 two Powder Mills blew up one after the other and in 2 minutes 4 more. Keith was killed and Drew died at noon.* [July 24, 1877] *Powder Mills blew up killing Charles Perry. I was standing talking with Puffer at the time in front to W.D. Brown's house—It was the sharpest report I ever heard—it knocked bricks off the chimney of Brown's little house and threw down dishes in our house.* [November 3, 1877]

According to historian Renee Garrelick, when Addison Fay, the general manager of the Massachusetts Powder Mills died in a March 1873 incident, Edward Damon was a pallbearer.

According to some sources, these were buildings of the powder mill. *Maynard Town Archives.*

An explosion in 1878 in which two workers were killed was one of the earliest and most dramatic. A headline in the *New York Times* declared, "Two Men's Remains Scattered over Three Acres of Ground." The article reported that the blast broke windows in Acton and was heard as far away as Boston. Three mill buildings were destroyed, as was the company office. A foreman named Hooper found the gold ring of one of the men killed and that was the only means of identifying him.

Thirty tons of gunpowder blew up in 1889, killing Maynard resident Douglas H. Livingston, who left behind a wife and one child. The Livingstons had moved to Maynard only two years before from Xenis, Ohio. This explosion was heard as far away as Framingham. As he often did, Maynard town physician Dr. Rich dealt with the daunting task of recovering the remains. Benjamin Ingham was killed in an explosion in 1892. In 1908 there were three different explosions in a month, with the second accident claiming the lives of Thomas Carey, fifty-two, and Thomas Waterhouse, thirty-five.

On an early May morning in 1895, a series of three explosions killed Nelson Morton, fifty-three; Frederick Winslow, twenty-eight; Albert Estes, forty-five; Charles Estes, twenty-five; and Charles O'Neil, twenty-five. Pages from Albert Estes's Bible were found three miles from the mill, near the reformatory at Concord Junction. Explosions at the powder mill were so commonplace that an unspoken custom had developed over time: after any explosion, all uninjured employees would rush home, so that their families could be sure of their safety. A fire in the nearby woods caused by the May 1895 blasts hampered workers' efforts to reach their homes.

In 1905 nitroglycerine leaked from improperly stored dynamite, leading to an explosion that killed Charles W. Moore. W.H. Bent represented Moore's beneficiary in suing the American Powder Mills for damages, and Moore was found to be not at fault. The United States Cartridge Company hired Stanley Transportation Company to move gunpowder out of the powder house so that repairs could be made to it, and Moore was the driver of the wagon. The boxes of powder were to be loaded by others, who then would direct where the teams should be driven. At a safe distance, the horses were to be unhitched from the loaded wagons and sent to their stable, while the workmen repaired the powder house. When the repair work was finished the drivers, with the horses, were to return and move back the powder. Such was the plan.

The building was divided into two compartments, one used by United States Cartridge Company for the keeping of gunpowder alone, the other by American Powder Mills for the keeping a large quantity of each of gunpowder and dynamite. The two compartments were separated by a partition of open joists, about two inches apart. Nearly four weeks before the explosion that killed Moore, United States Cartridge Company employees observed that the floor in the other compartment was discolored by nitroglycerine leaking from the dynamite, and that it had spread through the partition. The United States Cartridge Company notified American Powder Mills on July 7 about the danger and requested it be remedied. Finally on July 29, arrangements were made to remove the discolored portion and to put in a new floor. The owners of the powder were the ones responsible for seeing that it was being removed properly to avoid its exploding.

An employee named Goodwin, knowing the danger, poured a liquid on the discolored area without removing the large quantity of dynamite and gunpowder that still remained. After applying this liquid, he began scrubbing the surface with a broom. Smoke arose and the general explosion followed. Goodwin was found to be grossly negligent.

Five years later, in 1910, the *New York Times* reported two explosions, one in August and one in October. In the first incident, three different mill buildings blew up separately, and an Italian night watchman was killed. This type of danger continued throughout the years, and out of necessity, the American Powder Mills found its own way to deal with the financial and public relations repercussions.

This wagon of the National Express Company would have been similar to that driven by Charles Moore for the Stanley Transportation Company. *Maynard Town Archives*.

A main office of the American Powder Division. *Maynard Town Archives.*

The agreed upon evidence stated that on February 20, 1915, Daniel Splaine, the husband of the plaintiff, was killed while in the employ of the first company called American Powder Mills, which was a Massachusetts corporation later dissolved. Mr. Hooper, the foreman who had found the gold ring of one of the men killed after the 1878 explosion, was in 1915 the superintendent of the mill. He made a deal with Splaine's widow, Nora. Hooper promised that the corporation would pay her a pension for the rest of her life, if she did not sue the corporation or remarry. Mrs. Splaine did not sue and she did not remarry. She received $8.25 a week from the time of her husband's death until August 1930, when the payments stopped. At first, her money had come to her in the form of checks from American Powder Mills. In 1926 Cellulose Products, Inc., bought the mills for cash, and Mrs. Splaine never noticed that the checks then came from that company. Three of the nine directors of American Powder Mills became directors in Cellulose Products, Inc., and most of the employees were retained. Cellulose Products, Inc., made major changes, including the building of an additional plant. Even so, Nora Splaine testified that she "never noticed any change in the sign on the mills." Some time around 1927, Cellulose Products, Inc., changed its name to American Powder Company.

In 1929 American Cyanamid Company bought the enterprise, and the company was run by an entirely new group of people. At this time Nora Splaine's pension, according to court documents, was listed among others as follows: "List of voluntary pensions paid by American Powder Company which may be discontinued at any time at the option of the American Powder Company. Name. Mrs. Splaine. Age. 65 years of age. Amount. $8.25 a week. Term. Term for life."

Mrs. Splaine received the checks from the ACC subsidiary called American Powder Company. The new American Powder Company continued to pay Nora Splaine's pension until August of 1930. When the checks stopped coming, Mrs. Splaine took the company to court. The company's records indicated that the pension was an optional payment that could be discontinued at the discretion of the company. Mr. Hooper, the company official who originally made the promise to Mrs. Splaine, had died in 1923. The judge ruled against Mrs. Splaine. Represented by H.E. Cryan and E.P. Shaw before judges Rugg, Crosby, Pierce, Field and Lummus, she appealed, but lost.

Hooper had died in 1923, and there were no other employees of American Powder Mills or Cellulose Products, Inc., who would say that Nora Splaine's pension was contractual. Mrs. Splaine herself never purported to have received anything other than her original promise from Hooper on behalf of American Powder Mills. But that promise was legally not enough to bind the company. In what some would say is typical legalese, the court ruled that in this situation "there is no room for the application of the principle that knowingly to lead a person reasonably to suppose that *you promise* and *to promise* are the same thing…Exceptions overruled." American Powder Mills was freed from giving Nora Splaine $8.25 a week.

Mrs. Splaine was not the only one for whom the new company tried to break its promises. On June 14, 1916, Thomas King was severely burned while working at the American Powder Mills. No one disagreed that the liability for the injury was on the American Powder Mills. The president and the superintendent of the powder mills visited King in the hospital, and they made an oral contract. King agreed not to sue and the mill officials agreed to give King "six days' pay a week plus all expenses that may incur through this accident, for life whether you are able to work or not, and in case of your death if you don't come out of this we guarantee to take care of your family."

As King said later, and quoted in the court documents,

I did not expect that I could sit still and not work the rest of my life. I expected as a result of that talk that I was to work when able at the American Powder Mills at all times when they had anything for me to do, except when I had to be away for treatments on account of the injury. In other words, when they said they were going to give me six days' pay a week I understood that unless I had to go to the hospital or see a doctor on account of my hands or they were in such pain that I couldn't work I was going to perform the work which they had for me to do at the plant, as far as I was able.

King eventually went back to work, and was employed until 1926.

When American Cyanamid Company bought the mill, it tried to get out of the agreement with King, but he took them to court. C.C. Steadman argued on King's behalf before the judges Rugg, Crosby, Pierce, Lummus and Qua. Four of these judges sat on the Nora Splaine case as well, and even though they were looking at the same corporate history, they arrived at the opposite ruling. The Superior Court awarded King damages of $18,491.90.

Why was Thomas King successful in suing the company while Nora Splaine was not? The promises made by the American Powder Mills to each were similar. Stranger still, while Nora Splaine's name appeared on the list of employees and employees' widows who were to be receiving money, Thomas King's name did not appear. The two cases were decided within three years of each other.

As the years went by, explosions continued, and at various points current events added a sinister aspect to them. On an otherwise quiet winter night in 1940, a two-mile area shook when the unexpected blast of a smokeless powder magazine tossed timbers hundreds of feet. The company at that time was called American Cyanamid and Chemical Corporation, and fortunately for them, this time there were no casualties. World events had put terrorism in the public mind, but although the press was anxious to hear it, officials and state police refused to discuss the possibility of sabotage. The next day a huge explosion occurred in a dynamite mixing plant in Gibbstown, New Jersey, reported by the *Los Angeles Times*. This New Jersey explosion was the second one in a period of less than twenty-four hours, involving plants in the industrial Northeast, so agents from the Federal Bureau of Investigation were ordered to the scene.

For such a seemingly quiet town, sabotage and terrorism had a surprisingly significant share of attention in Maynard. In point of fact, the town was a hotbed of radicalism, as the next chapter demonstrates.

Chapter 5

Bolsheviks and Wobblies

*F*rankly, back in the thick of the radicalism and labor disputes of the 1910s through the 1950s, Maynard was full of Bolsheviks and members of the Industrial Workers of the World (IWW or Wobblies). Sociologists and historians have explored the phenomenon of the "Finnish immigrant radicals," and Maynard was home to more than a few. Not to mention their neighboring Polish immigrant counterparts—one of whom named Stasiukevich found himself challenged at his 1948 petition for citizenship.

This story begins again with the Finns of Maynard. The first wave of Finnish immigration brought those for whom the church was an extremely influential institution. The church reinforced Finnish nationalism by keeping the immigrants in contact with their old parishes.

By 1910 there was a critical mass of Finns, so a Lutheran church was built on Glendale Street. In 1913 a Congregational church was built on Walnut Street. The Russian Orthodox church was built in 1917, with its European spires standing to this day on Prospect Court. This was the time of the Russian Revolution, and Russians were running the powder mill. By supporting churchly activities, these Finns and Russians could distinguish themselves from their more radical, non-churchgoing brethren. Recently in a conversation over coffee, Gloria Korsman described growing up in Maynard in a Finnish family. There was a strong philosophical split among the Finns in town. She characterized the two groups as the Lutherans and the Socialists.

Contact with the church in Finland was frequent, but with the polarization of the Finnish immigrant community between the churches and the Socialists in the twentieth century, the church increasingly started to stress loyalty to the United States. This became apparent during the time of the great strike waves of 1907, through the establishment of the anti-Socialist leagues. The issue of patriotism and loyalty was also prominent during and after World War I, when a dichotomy developed between Finnish Americans who worked toward contacts with the American community versus the revolutionary radicals who supported the ideals of the Russian Bolshevik Revolution.

The Socialist Finns were part of a later wave of immigration to the United States, and essentially were not visible before 1900. In 1924, 40 percent of the people in Finland were Socialist, and 25 percent of the Finns in America were. John Wargelin, in his book about the Americanization of the Finns, tries to give an explanation of the Finns who are Socialist, but it is a wan attempt, at best, on account of his perspective as a conservative "churchy" Finn. Wargelin says, "Socialism among many Finns can be traced to the political oppression that Finland has suffered at the hands of Russian autocrats."

The highest number of emigrants came first from the rural north of Finland. Later emigrants were the Socialists, who met with hostility or indifference from the earlier Finns. Hoglund, attributing the information to the Socialists, says these first arrivals created a "Gibraltar of conservatism" in the Cape Ann area of Massachusetts. While the early immigrant Finns (1900) were seen as desirable, with "unlimited capacities for work, thrift, frugality, temperance, piety, and obedience," the later Finns (1911 and later) were seen as Socialists, "demagogues and agitators," creators of labor unrest and disturbances. Yet ultimately, the Finnish Socialist Federation got support in Massachusetts. The Socialists were against the sentiment of nationalism because they saw it as a barrier to understanding and being conscious of class. At the same moment, according to Hoglund, the anti-Socialist Finns who were business owners, churchmen and temperance leaders, were forming leagues to promote the idea that, rather than Socialists and strikers, Finns were "Christian, law-abiding, hard workers."

Since some of the Socialists were strongly antiwar during World War I, the federal government watched them closely. Maynard saw its share of redbaiting and oppressive scare tactics. War Department agents, for example, searched the offices of *Raivaaja* ("Pioneer"), the Fitchburg Finnish Socialist daily newspaper, which had been publicizing controversial ideas such as that warmongering capitalists profited from government contracts. In 1914 the circulation of *Raivaaja* was eight thousand. The paper is still published, although now it identifies itself as being "a not-for-profit Finnish American Weekly."

During the Red Scare on May 31, 1918, two Maynard men, allegedly IWW members, were arrested. On August 2, 1918, four hundred subscriptions to *Raivaaja* were late arriving in Maynard because the government was inspecting the editorial office in Fitchburg. During the Palmer Raids, five Maynard homes were raided, with one arrest on the charge of promoting anarchy in January 1920. In part it was this strong harassment by the federal government that motivated the non-radical Finns to form the national Finnish American Loyalty League.

All immigrants to the United States, flanked by their old and new worlds, faced the tension between allegiance to their former home and assimilation to their new one. For the Finns, this tension between nationalism and Americanization was controversial in both the radical and conservative camps. A difference existed in the process of Americanization in church circles from that in the labor movement. The church Finns were "largely 'compelled' to assimilate," as Auvo Kostiainen puts it. "They were basically nationalistic, but the decision to favor 'loyalism' forced them to become more American." But they were concerned that the younger generation, effectively assimilated, would allow the Finnish American church eventually to become simply American.

Mill workers gathered. *Maynard Town Archives*.

The forces of Americanization were also at work within the radical movement. Douglas J. Ollila has said that because the IWW was a completely American organization, the Finnish Wobblies Americanized very rapidly. In the Socialist- and Communist-dominated Finnish consumer cooperative movement, Americanization also happened quickly because it emphasized contact with international and American cooperative movements. Communication in English among these groups was a necessity, particularly after World War II. Kostiainen suggests that the language barrier motivated a quick Americanization because once the Finnish language became of secondary importance, it was a slippery slope toward letting go of all Finnish cultural features.

The complicated dynamic is notable. Insularity of institutions worked against any trend toward assimilation. For example, the insularity of the Finnish church thrived despite the forces to Americanize. The insularity of the Finnish labor and political organizations remained strong despite the American-ness of the IWW as opposed to the internationality of the Bolsheviks and the Communists. The radical Finns, according to Kostiainen, were "exceptionally active in the political labor movement, although their activities stressed ethnic social functions in addition to political ones." This additional cultural activity made it particularly easy for them to think beyond the traditional attitudes of other groups of workers. These were workers who either did not organize at all, or else participated only in the "conservative" trade unions.

St. Bridget's Parochial Residence, Maynard, Mass.

St. Bridget's, one of Maynard's many churches, a vibrant thread running through the cultural life of the time. *Peg Brown.*

Raivaaja published the writings of Robert G. Ingersoll, a famous American agnostic. "Blatant and militant anti-clericalism," as Hoglund says, resounded on these pages. In 1907 "labor strikes separated churchmen and socialists more sharply than ever before." Eventually, churchmen grew stronger as the Synod, Apostolic and National Lutherans consolidated. Internal factions and "middle-class aspirations" weakened the Socialists, along with external factors, such as repression by employers and authorities.

Finnish American radicals first supported the Bolsheviks and the Russian Revolution of 1917, but as the Bolsheviks took control of Russia, some of the Finns—particularly those on the East Coast—began to disagree with what they were doing, and *Raivaaja* was "becoming increasingly critical of their actions," according to George Hummasti. The establishment of American Communism in 1919 made it more complex, as the radicals were no longer radical enough. Among Socialists, a split occurred over industrial unionism—Social Democrats versus industrial union radicals.

The civil war in Finland lasted from January to May 1918. Russian Red Guards took over in Helsinki, the capital, and the Finnish government stayed in power in the western and northern parts of the country. Supporting the Red Guards were the Finnish American leftists and workers, while the Finnish American churchmen, the bourgeoisie, were on the side of the Finnish government. After the war ended, new arrivals from Finland were carefully assessed by Finnish Americans as to their allegiance during the war. The church Finns, according to Kostiainen, were after the "White," those who supported the Finnish government, in order to keep the Finnish reputation clean. The Finnish American workers' organizations, including the Communists, the IWW supporters and the Socialists, all in support of the "Red," wanted to keep their locals free of the "White" Finnish *lahtarit*, or "butchers."

In Michael M. Passi's summation, though promising in 1918, the "flourishing" working-class radical movement "had been seriously undercut as a living part of Finnish American cultural life," over the following two decades. "The Socialists, Wobblies, and Communists gradually became isolated figures in the Finnish-American communities which their uncompromising commitment to socialism, cooperation, and union organization had done so much to shape."

The Finns weren't the only radicals. Maynard hosted many Polish radicals as well, at least one of whom ran into trouble with the federal government. On January 20, 1947, a petition hearing came before the district court regarding the naturalization of a man named Stasiukevich. The lower court ruled against Stasiukevich's naturalization petition, but on appeal the ruling was reversed. Seen as a matter of naturalization and the interpretation of attachment to Constitutional principles, this case made the legal journals, again exemplifying Maynard as a quintessential locus of social issues.

Stasiukevich came from Poland in 1906 and settled in Maynard. In 1910 he married a woman who at some point became a naturalized alien. When asked by the court as to his occupation, he testified, "I examine cloth, and dry finish."

Since 1926 or 1928, he had been a member of the International Workers Order (IWO) and became an officer of the Maynard IWO lodge. A booklet containing the organization's declaration of principles, its constitution and bylaws was before the court as an exhibit. The organization described itself as a "people's fraternal benefit society." The court decided it "does not appear to indicate anything of a 'subversive' character in its professed aims and purposes."

The Maynard lodge met in a building owned by the Russian Educational Society. Stasiukevich and others held a mortgage on the building, which was known by some people as Red Hall. Stasiukevich had taught some Russian language classes in this hall. In 1933 he made a visit to Leningrad and Moscow, but he did not find life there to his liking.

From time to time, a group of people referred to by townsfolk as gypsies would camp on the outskirts of town, looking for temporary work and business opportunities. This photograph may be of that group, or may be others posing as them. *Maynard Town Archives*.

Stasiukevich denied being a member of the Communist Party and testified that he had "never advocated sabotage or the forceful overthrow of government." If he became a citizen he would "support the principles of the Constitution of the United States."

Lewis Marks, who worked as the assistant manager of a wholesale electric house in Boston called American Electric Supply, held the office of treasurer of the International Workers Order in the state of Massachusetts. Marks testified at the hearing that the IWO operated as a fraternal benefit society. According to him, IWO members were accepted "regardless of their race, creed, color or political affiliations." He allowed that since their political affiliation is not questioned, some IWO members might be Communists, but that the IWO "definitely is not Communistic, and operates on democratic principles."

Joseph S. Apelman, an immigration inspector, was the only witness offered by the Immigration Service in opposition to the petition. He testified that he had investigated Stasiukevich, by visiting Maynard and talking with fifteen or twenty neighbors.

The court as part of its direct examination asked Apelman, "What is Stasiukevich's reputation in the community?"

"His reputation in the community is of being a Communist," Apelman replied.

In further testimony, Apelman said he had also investigated the character of the International Workers Order. "I have studied," he said, "the report of the Special Commission to investigate the activities within the Commonwealth of the Communists, Fascists, Nazis, and other subversive organizations, so-called; also the report of the Special Committee on un-American activities, House of Representatives, Seventy-eighth Congress."

"Objection!" the counsel for Stasiukevich interjected. "Objection to this report, or series of reports, through the witness."

The court assured counsel that the government was going to offer the reports in evidence, and the examination proceeded. The court asked Apelman the question, "What was the general trend of the report of the Legislative Committee?"

Apelman at this point read "somewhat inaccurately" a couple of selected sentences from the report, which seemed to suggest that the aims and objectives of the International Workers Order were in synch with the whole of the Communist Party program. Apelman then quoted a brief excerpt from the report of the Congressional Committee. "The International Workers Order is a mere adjunct of the Communist Party." The two reports referred to were then introduced as exhibits.

It was understood by all at hand that naturalization could not be granted unless the petitioner "has been and still is a person of good moral character,

50

attached to the principles of the Constitution of the United States and well disposed to the good order and happiness of the United States." The judge on the appeals case, Magruder, was concerned that because a definition of "principles of the Constitution" was difficult to nail down exactly, its interpretation could be unfairly misused. In a rather prescient way of thinking, Magruder said,

> *The phrase goes back to the naturalization act of January 29, 1795. It is hardly to be supposed that the members of Congress of that day, having so recently completed a successful revolution, conceived that the phrase "the principles of the Constitution" comprehended only one principle, [but] that "if there is any principle of the Constitution that more imperatively calls for attachment than any other it is the principle of free thought—not free thought for those who agree with us but freedom for the thought that we hate."*

In 1918 Stasiukevich had claimed alienage exemption from the draft, under the Selective Service Act of the First World War. Magruder was concerned that the earlier court may have ruled that an alien who had been exempted from military service in time of war could not be "attached to the principles of the Constitution." Magruder was cautious, wondering if the court had decided that Stasiukevich's membership in the International Workers Order demonstrated his lack of attachment to the principles of the Constitution. The IWO was not found by the court to be an organization that "believes in, advises, advocates or teaches the overthrow by force or violence of the government of the United States." If the IWO was not for the overthrow of the government, it was wrong to deny naturalization. Equally wrong, according to Magruder, would be if the court was operating on the unspoken premise that Stasiukevich was a Communist. Apelman's testimony did not prove Stasiukevich's membership in the Communist Party because of the testimony of fifteen or twenty persons in Maynard. "This is hearsay of a particularly unreliable sort, in view of the loose and indiscriminate way in which the man in the street, and sometimes informed people who ought to know better, use the terms 'communist' and 'communistic.'"

Apelman was out of line in testifying, particularly over objection, "as to the conclusions drawn from his 'investigation' of the character of the International Workers Order." His understanding of the organization was limited entirely to what he had read in the two legislative reports. Apelman's testimony on the subject consisted merely of reading brief extracts from these reports. The report the court admitted was the report of the "Special

Commission to investigate the activities within this Commonwealth of Communistic, Fascist, Nazi and other subversive organizations, so called."

It was a detailed report on the "antecedents, organization, history, literature and activities of the International Workers Order and makes the following ultimate finding with reference thereto":

> *Without exception, the entire program of the Communist Party and of its fringe organizations is followed by the I.W.O. With the Communist Party it shares: Hatred of religion, hatred of American patriotism, building defense of the Soviet Union, the war against capitalism, and the campaign to involve all American workers in a class struggle for power.*

The report contained a similar recital of the structure, activities and program of the Communist Party, and found that the objective of the Communist Party of Massachusetts and of its affiliates "is to create a Soviet America, a dictatorship governed by a ruling caste constituting the Communist Party, as in Soviet Russia." The other report referred to and admitted in evidence is House Report No. 1311, 78th Congress, 2d Session, March 29, 1944, Report of the Special Committee on Un-American Activities. This report dealt mainly with the CIO Political Action Committee. In support of the thesis that the CIO Political Action Committee had a Communist tinge, the report referred to one of the national leaders of this organization as being closely affiliated with the International Workers Order as writer and speaker, adding that the International Workers Order "is a mere adjunct of the Communist Party."

It is odd that such an inflammatory report would be allowed in the hearing because it was so emotional and because Stasiukevich testified under oath that he was not Communist. Fortunately for Stasiukevich, Judge Magruder vacated the earlier denial of petition for naturalization and restored the possibility that the petition could ultimately go through.

Who were those fifteen or twenty Maynard residents who thought that Stasiukevich was a Communist, and how were they defining that word? Did Apelman invent them to support his case? If they were real, maybe what they meant by "communist" was that Stasiukevich belonged to one of Maynard's consumer cooperatives. The consumer cooperative movement was yet another side of Maynard's radicalism.

Chapter 6

SOCIALISM'S RISE AND FALL
Working People Take Charge of Their Consumer Power

Socialism used to be a vibrant thread running through the fabric of life in Maynard. For a hundred years, consumer cooperatives operating on Socialist principles dominated retail life in the town. Legend has it that the first store in Maynard in the mid-1800s was run as if it were a company store. Workers could buy on credit and have what they owed deducted out of their next paycheck from the mill, but prices at the store were extremely high. Many workers chose instead to walk three miles to the only other merchant.

An early attempt to remedy this situation was the Riverside Cooperative Association, formed in 1878. English and Irish immigrants, members of the Sovereigns of Industry, sold shares among the mill workers at five dollars each. They raised enough capital to open a store, a large three-story building near the mill, where they sold groceries, hardware, shoes, clothing, medicine, grain and even coal. By 1909 there were six hundred members. In 1882 the association built the four-story Cooperative Hall on the corner of Nason and Summer Streets, what is now the Knights of Columbus building. The first floor was a store, the second floor rooms, the third floor a meeting hall and the fourth floor a banquet hall. The building hummed with town meetings, rallies and social events until 1936, when fire destroyed the top two floors. The association, having seen business decline for decades, sold the building to the Knights of Columbus and disbanded.

The Finnish Socialists never felt quite welcome in the Riverside Society, in part because of the language barrier, so in 1906 the Finnish weavers and mill workers were taking a sauna at the bathhouse on River Street when they decided to form their own organization. In 1907 they founded the

Kaleva Society. It was firmly grounded in the group solidarity and Socialist philosophy of these particular Finns.

To guide their policies and practices, the consumer cooperatives used the seven Rochdale Principles, established in 1844 by the first consumer cooperative in Rochdale, England, called the Rochdale Society of Equitable Pioneers. The principles, according to Frank Aaltonen, are universality (open membership to all), democracy (one member, one vote), equity (limited interest paid on capital, and all profits returned to members), economy (cash trading at market prices), publicity (membership information and education), unity (cooperative movement as one the world over) and liberty (voluntary participation). The Kaleva Society members were dedicated to these principles.

Eventually the Kaleva Society changed its name to the United Cooperative Society (UCS), and in its heyday its operations included two food stores, a hardware department, a gas station, a baking plant, a pasteurization and bottling plant for dairy products and a restaurant. The society provided "soup kitchens" for picketers during strikes at the mill and gave free milk to schoolchildren during hard times.

The popular Finnish Social Hall stands overflowing with its membership. *Maynard Town Archives.*

Finns had a strong "associative spirit" and formed many organizations, including "congregations," temperance societies, benefit associations, choral groups, Socialist locals, library clubs and cooperative enterprises. Since Finland itself had been controlled by a state church, one of the freedoms the immigrants embraced was forming their own religious groups. These were mostly varieties of Lutherans—Apostolic, Synod and Evangelical—but they were also Congregational, Methodist and Baptist. Their organizations were dynamic, constantly changing based on personality differences, rifts and strong opinions. Factions withdrew and members formed rival associations, each determined to carry on every cultural practice. For example, nationally, the Finnish-American labor movement broke up into three quarrelling factions. There were the Socialists, the Wobblies (Industrial Workers of the World) and the Communists. There were some communities in which neither faction wanted to give up its dramatic society.

Regardless of their differences, their political stance (for or against Socialism) or their religious philosophy (staunchly Lutheran or not), all Finns supported the consumer cooperatives. In Maynard, for example, a third cooperative, the First National Cooperative Association, was established in 1915 by anti-Socialist Finns, who attended the Lutheran and Congregational churches and were otherwise conservative. These Finns considered the United Cooperative Society members to be atheists. This alternative cooperative society ran successfully for a decade or so, but it was never as active or successful as the UCS, and it went bankrupt in 1941. Shortly after the First World War, there was also a Polish cooperative society that lasted for about decade.

During the Depression, economic pundits marveled at Maynard's robust retail health, where the United Cooperative Society showed steadily increasing sales. In his book *Case Studies of Consumers' Cooperatives*, published in 1941, Professor Howard Haines Turner called it the largest store society in the East. The reasonable prices, the high quality of the merchandise and the high standard of service provided by the cooperative societies resulted in lower prices charged by all retailers in Maynard.

The experts agreed that the main reason consumer cooperatives were so successful in Maynard was the unique nature of the town. Half of Maynard's seven thousand residents were born in other countries, and among them they spoke fifteen different languages. "These cooperatives were built by radical groups within the wage-earning population," as Turner put it. He pointed out that each group was homogeneous, each one made up of foreign-born workers speaking one language. Encouraged by the success of other cooperatives, they managed to "evolve out of local leadership without outside support."

Music played an integral role in the cultural life of Maynard's Finns. The Women's Chorus was only one of several musical groups. *Maynard Town Archives*.

All was not entirely rosy, however. Professor Turner interviewed the Italian manager of a Tydol gas station on the corner opposite the cooperative's gas station. The disgruntled manager had lost a lot of his business to the cooperative, and he complained that their policies were deferential to their members. "If a Finn customer came into the store when you were buying anything they'd turn right around and wait on him first no matter how long you'd been there." A Polish grocer who had been losing business to the cooperative said that they were "Socialists and Anarchists and all kinds of fellows over there."

By 1929 the British founders of the Riverside Society had improved their economic situation significantly. At the mill they had become the supervisors and the middle management. Their children and grandchildren were going into the professions. The founders had moved quite far from their original cooperative ideals and the struggles that had motivated them. The Riverside Cooperative Society quietly faded away.

Average sales for all regular food stores together in Maynard in 1935 were $30,000, while in the same year the two cooperatives were each earning $100,000 in sales. The average sales for the six gas stations in town were $8,000, while the cooperative's gas station sales were $19,000.

The United Cooperative Society was so efficiently managed that it was able to expand its business to serve a large proportion of the non-Finnish population of Maynard. The cooperatives charged lower prices, and the consequent reductions in the prices charged by all retailers in Maynard benefited other consumers as well as the members of the cooperative society.

Above: This bottling plant indicates the cooperative was also on the forefront of industrial production technology. *Maynard Town Archives.*

Opposite: In its heyday, the United Cooperative Society was on the cutting edge of marketing and design. *Maynard Town Archives.*

The cooperative also brought in a higher quality of merchandise and a higher standard of service, effecting similar improvements among all the merchants in town. Unlike working in the privately owned stores, employees of the cooperatives were encouraged to take a mid-afternoon coffee break, a time-honored Finnish custom. The hours of work were shorter, and jobs were more secure in the cooperatives.

Their stylish service station illustrates the intertwining of interests between the cooperative and the corporate. *Maynard Town Archives.*

In the assessment of the experts, Maynard was a town dominated by an absentee corporation. Essentially an autocracy, the options for earning a living were narrow. In such a setting, the cultural contribution of a workers' cooperative society may have been more important than the material. Maynard's cooperative movement was a successful attempt by a group of the workers to make economical retail purchases without fear of exploitation. Consumers' cooperation did not, however, change the town's reliance on the American Woolen Company.

After World War I, immigration from Finland virtually ceased, not only because the United States was strictly enforcing new immigration quotas, but also because many of the pressures to leave Finland had diminished. This situation meant the supply of Finland-born Maynardians was finite. By the late 1970s, the United Cooperative Society did still own four stores, a bakery, a dairy and continued to handle grain, coal and oil.

Turner's analysis of the Maynard cooperatives suggests that the barrier between the Finns and the non-Finns seemed to become firmer as the immigrant Finns grew older and "the early members of the society became increasingly occupied with the question of maintaining Finnish control." Their children were another story, as they took the cooperatives for granted. As Gloria Korsman, who grew up in Maynard said, "The co-ops were the norm." To these American-born children, language was not a barrier, but the cooperative ideals in themselves simply did not hold much vitality. As for the strongest of the co-ops, the United Cooperative Society, Professor Turner wrote in 1941, the "'clannishness' of the Finns, which probably promoted the development of the cooperative society in the first place, subsequently proved a limiting factor. Social prejudice—against other nationalities and against radical philosophies—restrained non-Finnish people from supporting the cooperative. The critical question of cooperative success after the foreign-born members are gone is yet to be answered." Time has now answered that question: the cooperative societies have all but disappeared.

Chapter 7

MAYNARD FEUDS OVER INTOXICATING LIQUORS
Battle of Village Morality

*O*n the south side of Main Street, at the corner of River Street in Maynard, an innkeeper named Clark and prominent local businessman Bartholomew J. "B.J." Coughlin intended to build an inn. On March 25, 1908, Clark first applied to the selectmen of the town for a license as an inn holder and for a liquor license. At that moment, there was no building on the lot and none being constructed. The public notice of the application properly appeared, and on March 31 the work of digging the cellar for the inn began. With no apparent objection from the general public, the board of selectmen decided unofficially on April 15 that they would grant a license to Clark when the building was completed. The inn holder's license would allow Clark to be an inn holder at 34–36 Main Street; the liquor license would allow him to sell, as legal jargon called it, "intoxicating liquors."

Construction progressed, with the foundation and cellar ready by April 28 for the superstructure of the building. By May 22, although the building was not nearly finished, it was far enough along and well enough furnished that a small number of strangers and travelers could be fed and lodged. On May 22 Clark applied once more for a license, and on that day the selectmen officially granted an inn holder's license and a liquor license. The inn was completed on June 27, 1908. The official history books report it now quite simply: "In 1909 B.J. Coughlin built the Somerset Hotel at the corner of Main and River streets." The short sentence does not begin to suggest the controversy that surrounded the episode.

B.J. Coughlin seems to have been a self-styled cultural impresario in town. Among other things, he was very involved in the new business of movies. There was a surprising amount of competition between film venues in

Coughlan's substantially successful Livery Feed and Sale Stable anchored the wide-ranging Coughlan business enterprises. *Maynard Town Archives.*

1909, the same year he was completing his hotel. Coughlin's Music Hall and the Riverside Cooperative Hall juggled for position. In 1914 Coughlin opened the new Colonial Hall on Main Street for film, showing movies several nights a week. In 1921 People's Theatre opened on Nason Street. By the mid 1940s, only People's Theatre remained, run by Burton J. Coughlan. Sources suggest Burton Coughlan was the son of B.J. Coughlin, and he appears to have adopted a variant spelling of their last name. In 1949 Coughlan opened the Fine Arts Theatre, said by Gutteridge to be built on the site of his father's former livery stable and garage.

The court files suggest that not everyone appreciated B.J. Coughlin's involvement in so many facets of Maynard culture. As the work on his new hotel progressed, ten concerned citizens of Maynard, led by Charles H. Cheney, a town founder, became alarmed at the notion of the availability of alcohol at the new hotel. They got together and sued to restrain Coughlin's business partner Clark from using the building as an inn and for the sale of intoxicating liquors. As the court documents put it, the concerned citizens "prayed for its abatement as a common nuisance."

The temperance movement had long been active in town, in the form of organizations such as the Finnish Alku Temperance Society and St. Bridget's Catholic Temperance and Benevolent Society. At the same time, drinking was still popular. A September 1901 issue of the *National Police Gazette*, for example, featured a sketch of Billie Campbell of the Maynard House as one of its "prominent saloonmen," a column that appeared regularly and featured for free any saloonman, hotel keeper or bartender who sent in his photograph. "Jovial Billie Campbell," it said, "is an all around sport, a thorough good fellow in every respect, and he is furthermore the very popular bartender behind the bar at the Maynard House. He has held this position for fifteen years and has always mixed the best of drinks and given good satisfaction to the patrons of the establishment. He has a host of friends in and around Maynard, and as a mixologist it is safe to say that Billie is in a class all by himself." The friends of Billie Campbell were likely not friends of Charles Cheney and his "ten concerned citizens."

The concerned citizens brought suit to restrain the use of the building for the sale of alcohol, and the Supreme Judicial Court considered the issue. The presiding judge found it "highly irregular and unwarranted" that Clark, on March 25, would describe, in his original application to the selectmen of the town, a building that did not yet exist.

The court documents specify that to determine if certain conditions are met the building must have a "real and corporeal existence." For example, one can object to granting a license if the building is "ill adapted for use as an inn," which often means that the applicant could be using an "inn" as a cover, just to get the liquor license, with the sale of liquor being the main business. Another common objection is when the building is too close to a school. You could only measure a "genuine building, and not one resting only on the imagination." In order to determine if the screens, shutters, and stained glass windows are within the law, a building must "be on the face of the earth."

Maynard Feuds Over Intoxicating Liquors

The final word of the court was that no valid license could be granted upon a building that doesn't exist. Of course, by the time the court made its decision, the building did exist and could have been easily measured and assessed. Founder C.H. Cheney won that battle, but Clark and Coughlin's inn eventually became today's Pleasant Café.

This series of photos suggests the breadth of commerce in Maynard. *Top to bottom:* Middlesex Hotel and Assabet House; then the Amory Block with a barber shop, cigar store and hardware store, with apartments above; and finally a pool room, Maynard Coal Company and a photo studio on the upper level. *Maynard Town Archives.*

Opposite: The Riverside Block on Main Street hosted much of Maynard's activity through the years. *Maynard Town Archives.*

Intoxicating liquors continued to be a contentious issue over the years, even before Prohibition was in effect. By 1915 Maynard's laws regarding alcohol were highly restrictive, and Frank S. Binks, the police chief and chairman of the board of selectmen, may have used those laws to his advantage. In 1917, Binks was arraigned for taking bribes, accused of accepting money in exchange for keeping quiet about people's personal stashes of beer and whiskey. Possessing alcohol for personal use was not illegal, but intending to sell it without a license was. Binks allegedly exploited people's fear of being charged with intent to sell, and he received hush money. Binks and his high-powered attorneys apparently fought off the bribery charge, as two years later Binks turns up in the news again, still a selectman, involved in resolving the labor dispute at the mill in December 1919.

Chapter 8

MAYNARD AND THE "FAMILY"
Black Hand, Mafiosi

While it may look like a quiet little mill town, safely ensconced in the isolation of apple orchards and housing workers with their noses to the grindstone, Maynard has always maintained strong connections to the wider world, with fruitful and illuminating results through pollination of immigrant creativity and cosmopolitanism and radical political thought. The connections have not always been positive, however, and in fact, Maynard residents have, at various times, appeared to have links with organized crime, particularly in neighboring Waltham and in Brooklyn, New York.

Before Lieutenant Joseph Petrosino of the New York Police Department was murdered in Palermo in 1909, he had been quite outspoken on the subject of criminals in the United States from Italy.:

> *The United States has become the dumping ground for all the criminals and banditti of Italy, Sicily, Sardinia, and Calabria. A little over a year ago [1907] the Government officials of Tunis decided to clean out the Italian quarter of that city on account of the great number of crimes that were being committed there. A rigid investigation was conducted by the French Government, and as a result over 10,000 men were deported. Where did they go to? Uncle Sam received them with open arms. Nearly every one of them came to this country, and they are now thriving on the spoils of their blackmailing and other conspiracies.*

The *New York Times* often identified the Black Hand with criminal activity in the Italian American community in New York.

Giuseppe "Joe" Petrosino, born in 1860 near Salerno in Naples, arrived in New York City the age of thirteen. He joined the New York Police Department in 1883, and became an expert in Italian crime. Thomas Reppeto, a former police officer, has written extensively about organized crime. Reppeto says Petrosino was aware of the useful distinctions among Sicilian and Neopolitan families, who lived around Elizabeth Street and Mulberry Street, respectively, and the families originally from the Italian village of Cinisi, who lived around East Sixty-ninth Street. Petrosino was promoted to lieutenant in 1907, and put in charge of a special Italian squad of twenty-seven men because of the "deluge of Black Hand cases." Despite this, Petrosino believed that there was no single Black Hand, or Mafia, but rather "small bands of Sicilians, Neapolitans, or Calabrians in the various towns." He believed they had their own little projects going on, some of which were union related. What might this have to do with Maynard?

According to the *New York Times*, Giuseppi Rizzo was shot and killed in a gang fight in Maynard on June 15, 1919. One man was convicted of the murder, and was serving a twenty-year term in prison, but the other man wanted in the crime, Giuseppi Cipollo, was on the lam.

An early twentieth-century view of Maynard's police force. *Maynard Town Archives.*

The police had sent out a general alarm for Cipollo, forty years old, of 17 Central Avenue, Tenafly, New Jersey, but no one had any photographs of him. Police did have, however, a photograph of his sister, Rose, to whom he bore a striking resemblance. The police used the photograph of his sister, retouched the hair to make it resemble that of a man and created a man's collar and coat. This photograph, along with a general description of the wanted man, went out to police all through the East.

When Hamilton Avenue Station's Detective Vincent Giordano learned that Gatano Caterasso was Cipollo's father-in-law, he began keeping a watch on the Caterasso home at 623 Union Street, Brooklyn. During this time, Caterasso died, and Giordano attended the funeral in the home. Afterward, he went to the cemetery with the mourners. There he recognized Cipollo from the retouched photograph. As Cipollo knelt at the grave of his father-in-law in Holy Cross Cemetery in Brooklyn, Giordano arrested him.

Cipollo admitted that he fired a shot in the fight with Rizzo and the gang but denied he was the actual murderer. The *New York Times* reported that "the prisoner has a wife and child living in Tenafly. They were not with him when he was arrested." One might wonder why the daughter was not attending the funeral of her father, and yet Cipollo, the son-in-law, was. Could Cipollo have been closer to Caterasso than his own daughter? If so, why?

Downtown Maynard during the "gangland" years. *Peg Brown.*

Other nefarious goings-on reverberated through Maynard at the time, including an event that may or may not have been related:

Two boys, paddling about on a raft in the Charles River near Waltham in March of 1919, found a floating body. When police examined the body, they found clues indicating that possibly the man had been a resident of Maynard. Gold-bowed glasses bore the name of a Maynard optician named Peel, and a railroad ticket from Waltham to South Acton rested in one of the man's pockets. Police gave this information to Mrs. Luigi Graccela, 7 High Street, as her husband of only ten days had been missing from home for two months. She went to Waltham early the next day and identified the body as that of her husband.

After the medical examiner performed an autopsy and found several knife wounds, one on the face, one on the hand and several in the chest, he determined the case to be one of murder. District Attorney Tufts took over and immediately made a link to the murder of Salvatore Parissi, which occurred in Waltham in 1917. Vincinzo Graccela, a cousin of Luigi Graccela whose body was found in the river, was convicted of killing Parissi and was serving an eighteen-year sentence. Police arrested Dominic Parissi in Fitchburg. Dominic Parissi and his brother, Angelo, were indicted for murder in Maynard a year before, and Angelo was sentenced to a year in prison.

Three Maynard residents in 1914. *Maynard Town Archives.*

The authorities believed that the Graccela murder was one of an epidemic of vendetta killings that had been revolving through the Italian communities in several cities and towns in Massachusetts.

The newspaper article describes the crime as a gangland murder. Was Maynard once gang-infested, home to elements of what would soon be known as the Mafia? What was the Mafia at the time and how was Maynard connected to it? Were these figures "collateral damage" in some bigger undercover investigation? It seemed that there was an unending chain of murders, a chain that remains difficult to follow because of secrecy and confusion. Many sources have spelled the names of the perpetrators and the victims more than one way, even within the same newspaper article. There may have been even more gangland violence than the newspapers identified. For example, a strange "accident" at the Assabet Mill was never connected to the Italian gangs. In an odd coincidence, Main Street and the dye house at the American Woolen Company were common threads in the deaths of both John Cinno in 1916 and Rosari Bascemi in 1923. Bascemi, of Butler Avenue, who worked in the checking room and dye house, was linked to a network of rival family grudges and feuds, and his death was believed to be a result of a gang fight at 133 Main Street. John Cinno lived at 111 Main Street and normally worked in a different department, but was temporarily assigned to the dye house. There he had the misfortune of being scalded to death in a vat of boiling water. While no one suggested Cinno was pushed against his will into the vat, the *Boston Globe* did say that company officials were at a loss to explain his jumping in.

Chapter 9

DIVERTING THE WATER
Building the Mill

*R*iparian—a word not often used to describe Maynard, but one that is quite apt. From the Latin word *ripa*, meaning "bank," riparian can describe anything that is on or near the bank of a river, stream, lake, sea or ocean. Lawyers have been very fond of the word, arguing at length over riparian lands, non-riparian landowners and degrees and variations of riparian rights, even making a distinction between navigable and non-navigable streams. Courts have disagreed about what qualifies as being on the bank. In this country, land is riparian to a particular flowing water if it is within the watershed, or even if it is on a slough that feeds the water during certain seasons. While such fine-tuned definitions may seem overly occupied with minutiae, oddly enough, the economic viability of towns have been determined by it, and Maynard is one of those towns.

Maynard's existence, its fundamental identity—like it or not—has relied on being a mill town. The water that flows past in the Assabet River has never been not private property, and the establishing of a mill was initially all about acquiring the water rights to ensure a stable source of power from the river. As the Massachusetts Court put it in 1910, "there is no right of property in such water in the sense that it can be the subject of exclusive appropriation and dominion…The right of each riparian owner is to have the natural flow of the stream come to his land and to make a reasonable and just use of it as it flows through his land." One owner's riparian rights stopped where those of any other owners began, above or below, on the river.

Amory Maynard set out to acquire every water right he could get, beginning with his purchase of land in May 1846. He continued to buy up all available water power, water rights and mill sites on both sides of the Assabet River. Soon he had control of the water rights up the river to Boon Lake in Stow and to Fort Meadow Pond in Marlborough. Amory began altering the landscape to improve his control of the water. He "dug a canal," and, as Gutteridge described it, "led the water to…a low swampy hollow with a trout brook running through." He cleared out trees and built the Ben Smith Dam.

Above: One of the earliest representations of the town, 1879. *Maynard Town Archives.*

Right: Of all the property he owned, Amory Maynard lived in this house. *Maynard Town Archives.*

The second edition of Joseph K. Angell's *A Treatise on the Common Law, in Relation to Watercourses* was printed in 1833. Between the years of the first edition in 1824 and the second, "more decisions probably were rendered on the subject of water rights…than all of an antecedent date put together." The years between these editions exhibited dramatic growth in textile manufacturing and factory villages. Accompanying the growth of factories, which were almost universally powered by water, there was an increase in court cases pertaining to water rights. The rights to water were integral to early industrialists. Water turned mill wheels, and it was also necessary in many manufacturing processes. This situation pitted factory owners against one another in the struggle for water power. Damming rivers for waterwheels caused a variety of problems for landowners along rivers. In some cases, the cotton mills released water from a reservoir upstream, flooding the mowing lot of a local farmer. Maynard saw its own share of these types of disputes.

Angell's *Treatise* described a decision that clearly set the tone for whose interests took precedence:

> *Under the statues of flowage in Massachusetts, it has been determined, that a mill owner is authorized to create a reservoir of water for the use of his mill, by erecting a dam remote from that at which the mill is situated, and the owner of land lying between the two dams, which is overflowed by the water from the reservoir, must apply for damages in the mode provided by the statutes. This decision was made in* Wolcott Manufacturing Company v. Upham, *in 1827.*

In 1847 the Assabet Mills started making carpet yarn, then carpets. In 1862 it reorganized into Assabet Manufacturing Company, expanded and switched from carpets to cloth and blankets for the Civil War. By 1868 the company became insolvent and went into receivership.

In receivership, the company made for a prime target. Benjamin W. Gleason took the opportunity to sue for rights to the mill. The court case, with its minute detail, illustrates well not only the perspective of the time period, but also the essential fabric of life in the river valley at that time.

Gleason's mill was built on the bank of the river, near the edge. Water from the wheel of the mill was discharged through an artificial raceway, which had been dug some time before 1847, from the wheel-pit through the bank of the river. Opposite the river from where this artificial raceway discharged, and for some distance above and below, was a natural island in the river. The water of the river would flow over a part of the island when the water was high, and so, some years before 1847, the people from whom Gleason bought the mill made a dam or breakwater from the bank above the outlet of the raceway to the upper part of the island. This dam prevented the water of the river from running down between the island and the bank where Gleason's mill stood.

Gleason owned most of the island. After the dam or breakwater was built, the river did not flow between the island and Gleason's mill, so, except for leaks, the only water flowing there was that discharged from Gleason's raceway. It came down to what might be called the Battle of the Flashboards: Gleason had a mill upstream from Assabet Manufacturing Company and wanted to change the streambed to get more power.

From the time the Assabet Manufacturing Company built their dam to the summer of 1850, the mill used flashboards, varying from six to twenty-one inches in width, to raise the water two feet or more. The Assabet Manufacturing Company believed that the raising of the water by the flashboards did little, if any, damage to the Gleason mill and did not adversely affect the working of the mill or the operation of its wheel.

The parties went into arbitration and agreed that if the court found that Gleason was right, the flashboards would have to be at most seven inches wide; if Assabet Manufacturing Company was right, the flashboards could then be as wide as twenty-one inches.

Could that be Gleason himself, surveying his mill and island from Summer Hill's pinnacle? *Maynard Town Archives.*

Gleason argued that a wheel was in his mill at the time Assabet Manufacturing Company built its dam, and "that no owner below on the same stream had any right to raise the water by a dam, or by flashboards on a dam, to such height as would cause the water to set back so as to impede or interfere with the full and perfect operations" of the Gleason wheel. Gleason believed he had the right to improve the natural bed of the stream used as a raceway. He should be able to widen the channel and remove all obstructions to deliver the water as needed.

By contrast, the Assabet Manufacturing Company believed they had the right to harness for their mill all the power of the river, up to the point to the injury to Gleason's older mill. If the present Gleason mill could not increase its water power except by deepening or widening their raceway, that was not Assabet Manufacturing Company's problem.

Despite Gleason's argument that the raceway was a branch of the stream, wholly on his own land, and that he had the lawful right to make any improvements in it he saw fit to facilitate the flow of the water from his wheel, the court was not convinced. Even though all Gleason wanted to do was remove obstructions and make only changes that would allow the water to flow as it did in 1847, the court ruled in favor of Assabet Manufacturing Company in order to enable them to use all the water power to which they were entitled. The court said that Gleason was entitled to the full benefit of all the water power he had appropriated originally, but was not entitled to make an additional appropriation of power by lowering or changing the natural bed of the stream below the mill.

A view of Maynard during the Industrial Revolution. *Peg Brown.*

Diverting the Water

As legal scholar John F. Hart has pointed out, rulings like this benefited the entrepreneurs who relied on building or improving water-powered mills, at the expense of landowners. "State intervention in this zero-sum bargaining situation lowered the cost of land for the entrepreneur, at the expense of the neighboring landowner." Over the years, the "incremental incorporation of a principle of priority" in favor of industrialists, during a time of increasing rivalry in the use of water power, was crucial in the development of vibrant mill towns. It was "essentially absolute protection to existing mills from all innovations in water usage affecting them, either from new mills or from modification of existing mills." The decision of the Massachusetts Supreme Court in favor of Assabet Manufacturing Company significantly strengthened the Company's economic position against its competitors, and coming as it did in 1869, it may have been a factor in the decision of the townspeople to incorporate Maynard as a town in 1871.

As a town, Maynard faced its own troubles with water-related controversy. In 1893 Arthur Howland actually sued all of the "inhabitants of Maynard" for libel. Maynard had hired a firm to construct a system of waterworks. Arthur Howland was a member of that firm. The alleged libel was contained in the report of an investigating committee appointed by the town. At a regularly called town meeting, the report was read, and the town voted to accept and adopt it and to have it printed and circulated. Following the meeting, the town clerk delivered the report to a newspaper published in a neighboring town. The report was printed in an extra edition of several hundred copies of that paper and circulated. The chairman of the town water commissioners ordered five hundred copies of the report printed and taken to the annual town meeting and distributed there, with all of the regular town reports.

The investigating committee had discovered and stated in the report that Arthur Howland had acted in bad faith, attempting to construct cheaper pumps than the specifications required. Initially Howland won his suit, but he lost on appeal. The court decided Howland couldn't simply sue the whole town for libel.

The court determined that towns are instituted for "political purposes, for convenience in the administration of the government...Their powers are special and limited...they are purely public and common to all towns, such as the maintenance of police, health, schools, and highways." There are so many matters of local concern that towns must act on that are special to the town's inhabitants. Things like waterworks, gas or electric lighting, free baths, the maintenance of main drains and common sewers, are for the general benefit of all the inhabitants of the particular town. Everything relating to them should be "subject to the action and consideration of the voters of the town duly assembled in town meeting. And whatever is done at such a meeting is done by the town in a legislative capacity and as a political body."

How could Arthur Howland try to sue an entire town, young and old, for libel? *Maynard Town Archives*.

The business of the town requires that meetings and the reports they generate must be public. A town must be free to print and publish reports in whole or in part, without fear that any individual voted upon, or mentioned in a report of a committee, would sue for libel. For good measure, the court noted "it would seriously impair the freedom of investigation which is often required in the proper conduct of municipal affairs if cities and towns were held liable to be sued in actions of libel."

So, for this time anyway, Maynard and its citizens were off the hook, at least from being sued. As described in the next chapter, the inhabitants of the town then faced a different kind of threat.

Chapter 10

SELLING THE MILL
Closures and Property Sales

$\mathcal{M}$aynard was not the only town along the Assabet River to host a mill. Concord's Damon Mill carried on a lively business exchange with the nearby Assabet Mills. Edward Carver Damon wrote in his diary, "Sent some wool to Assabet to be colored" and "Mr. Maynard was down to see if we could make them some woolen yarn…Went to Assabet to see Maynard and told him we would spin five bales of cotton for him at 15 cents per lb. of yarn." As historian Renee Garrelick phrases it, "powered by the same river source, the economic fortunes of both mills paralleled each other, the prosperity of the Civil War, the setbacks from the Depression of 1893 and the bankruptcy of both mills in 1898."

Garrelick sees Maynard's dependency on the mill as far greater than Concord's. Unlike Concord, Maynard had no banks, and in the early years the five hundred Assabet workers deposited their savings with the company. "While the disillusioned and angry townspeople were contemplating changing the name of their town back to Assabet, a rebirth occurred the following year when the American Woolen Company bought the Assabet Mills and furthered its expansion."

The Damon Mill's story took a bit sadder turn than Maynard's, but it ended up as happy. The Damon Mill closed at end of the century, and by that point New England had lost its dominance in clothing manufacture. It was 1923 when the Strathmore Worsted Mills closed after two decades of occupancy in the former Damon Mill, putting an end to the last use of the mill for textile manufacturing. The next concern to take residency was an apple and cold storage facility. By the mid-1970s, the buildings had deteriorated, essentially abandoned. After some local people became concerned and called for the mill's demolition, the Mill Square Partnership purchased the site in the fall of 1977. At that point the long struggle that many mill towns have faced began, with the goal of working toward small, diversified, owner-occupied commercial use. In 1980 the Damon Mill was on the National Register of Historic Places.

Edward Damon's prominence and involvement with the big personages of nineteenth-century New England and America could not stop his mill from dying. Damon was a director of the Middlesex Institution for Saving and the Concord National Bank. He was on the committee to design and build a public almshouse. He socialized with Concord's well-known transcendentalist writers and artists—Bronson Alcott, William Ellery Channing, Ralph Waldo Emerson and Henry David Thoreau. But once the bell tolled, none of them could help.

For Maynard's American Woolen Company, labor issues caused the early brushes with closing, rather than sales, for business was booming. These temporary closures in the first two decades of the twentieth century were short-lived, usually lasting only a few days. In 1901 a backlog of work in the mending department motivated Amory Maynard to bring in ten menders from Lawrence at ten dollars a week. The thirty young women menders already working there were paid only six to eight dollars a week. They went out on strike, demanding at least nine dollars, forcing the mill to close briefly. In November of 1907, the *Wall Street Journal* reported that the Assabet Mills had closed temporarily in a similar situation, putting about three thousand men and women out of work.

In 1920 there was an inkling of changing times when American Woolen Company President William M. Wood cautioned that competition was forcing him to consider cutting wages. Then in 1930 the *Wall Street Journal* reported that American Woolen Company's Assabet Mills would be suspending operations when present orders were run out. Going on to describe the Assabet Mills as the largest woolen mill in the world, with 700 looms and 55,000 woolen spindles, the *Wall Street Journal* qualified the report by noting that "in recent years the management has been scaling down operations until the mill is more nearly a 400-loom than 700-loom unit. Since the first of the year operations have been falling off, and at present the mill is running no better than 20% of capacity, on which basis profitable operation is impossible. Taxes levied on the property account for approximately 60% of the total collected in Maynard."

It was at this time the company decided to sell off its company-owned residential property.

The company-owned village was a common feature anywhere near a mill. The reason, according to Harriet Herring, is simple:

Unlike many mill towns, industrialization did not turn Maynard into an inhospitable wasteland. This image suggests that the preservation of the trees and the prominent placement of the church in the early years of the industrial movement may have helped. *Peg Brown.*

> *In the factory system which machinery ushered in, three elements were needed in abundance—capital, power, and labor. Before the day of electricity and railroads, power was the least mobile. The English mills were built at the rapids of rivers where there were few workers to be had from the sparse rural population. Operatives brought or attracted from elsewhere had no means with which to build homes, and investors in rental property had not yet found this new opening. The mills had to provide housing.*

The mill village usually comprised a few houses, a little school, a small church, a handful of families and an owner-manager. The tone of the village would be set by this individual, who would run the mill and community kindly or otherwise as he was inclined.

The improvement of urban and interurban transportation in New England meant that the mills did not have to provide houses. At the same time the better housing standards made maintaining the houses increasingly expensive. Federal legislation on wages made the higher expenses a competitive disadvantage. "Finally," as Herring says, "a new generation of mill managers had largely replaced the generation of old mill owners. Efficiency of management was now more fashionable than the paternalism of ownership." From this confluence of factors emerged a new phenomenon—"the break-up of the village by sale of the houses."

Selling the Mill

Two factors influenced the popularity of this movement—the textile code under the National Recovery Act of 1933, and President Roosevelt's suggestion that the if the mills dispose of their villages, regional wage differentials and other social problems could be solved. A committee appointed to study the idea was overwhelmed and baffled by the complexity of making it happen, but writers in the trade papers proposed various solutions. The one considered most practical was first the mills close or change hands, then an operating company comes in for the sale.

There were many good reasons for the mills to sell off their houses, including costs, equitability of the company toward the workers and encouraging stability in the workers via home ownership. Not only that, but the mill village paternalism was also not as necessary as it once might have been, and in fact was beginning to be resented. One of the most persuasive ideas, that homeownership would make more responsible citizens and better communities, began to take on a life of its own.

Still, Herring found that the first reaction of the tenants to the decision of the mill to sell was often shock. Workers said things like, "It was just like a bombshell" or "This village has never been in such a commotion." When asked why people are so surprised when the company has sold villages at other plants, one of the mill workers said, "Well, it's like death or an automobile accident—it can happen to the other fellow but not to you. We just *knew* the company wouldn't sell this village."

Once the mill announced the sale, the rumors flew. Some people were highly suspicious and thought the company must have had a hidden agenda. Herring found such rumors as "the mill will sell the house but not the lot, that it will retain a strip of land along the front of the lot, that it cannot or will not give a good title to the property, that it will 'fix some way to get the houses back.'"

Some tenants thought the sale would make it easier for the mill to lay off workers in dull times. Others thought just the opposite, that the homeowners will be laid off first because they are more likely to stay.

Rumors spread that the mill was going to close, or it was trying to keep out or weaken the union.

The sales went on, and despite their reservations, people bought the houses. As Herring describes it, "the purchasers immediately feel the release from the renter-transient psychology. Many a family had lived for years in a house, but they always 'might move.'" Now, because they will be staying, they start caring for their houses.

Herring found that everyone noticed this phenomenon, including school leaders and social workers, along with the mill management and the workers themselves. The new homeowners made many changes to the houses, including landscaping, painting, adding window treatments and siding.

They put up Venetian blinds and resurfaced the kitchen and bathroom floors with linoleum. They put in brick sidewalks and steps, added a bathroom, rewired, reroofed and reheated, all in an effort to make their own home individually distinct.

Several of the properties owned by the American Woolen Company prior to the real estate divestiture in the 1930s. *Maynard Town Archives.*

Selling the Mill

The American Woolen Company found itself facing the option of selling its village when the Depression hit. The company had built "160 tenements" with "their own sewerage system" and Presidential street names, when business expanded and more workers were needed in 1901–02. Then, in 1934 the American Woolen Company took the huge step of selling its mill houses at auction. Most houses were bought by the tenants who were mill employees.

After the housing sell-off, Maynard settled down once again. The new homeowners improved their property, the years passed and then in 1941, the mill began flourishing once again, around the clock, making cloth for the U.S. military. At this World War II peak of activity, the twenty-two-plant mill employed fifteen hundred workers, producing ninety thousand blankets a week. This high was only the precursor to the next low.

On the left is one of the mill's "tenement" houses, next door to Lorenzo Maynard's home on the right. *Maynard Town Archives.*

Below: The heart of the town in the glow of the moon, summoning dreams from the workers within. *Peg Brown.*

The press reported that finally the economic handwriting on the wall had come to be, and that Maynard was facing the liquidation of its mill. In 1950 American Woolen Company closed the mill, in part because the soft woolens made there were out of fashion, hard woven worsteds were the rage. An organization of citizens tried to buy the mill, but their offers were rejected. At this point, the mill had been the major employer for 108 years, and almost one-sixth of Maynard's 7,500 residents would be rendered jobless by the American Woolen Company's decision. Only 300 workers remained after the company's previous lay-offs.

The *New York Times* reported that the public was understandably angry with the company for its decision, "but regional economists have pointed out that the mill actually was a casualty of the shifting public taste in textiles." The tastes of the fickle public, and their demands for hard twist woolens rather than the soft weaves made at the Assabet Mill, were really to blame for the situation. A citizens' committee, headed by chairman of the Board of Selectmen Leo F. Mullin, was formed and was optimistically hoping to to set up a community corporation to buy the mill property. Then, similar to what Nashua, New Hampshire, did when Textron, Inc., closed down operations there two years before, the Maynard committee planned to lease out the available 2,250,000 square feet of space to new, diversified enterprises.

"We're in the same position as the man whose house was flattened by a hurricane," the *New York Times* quoted Mr. Mullin as saying. "There isn't anything to do but pitch a tent and weather out the storm, then start building a new foundation." Mayor Hugh Gregg of Nashua came to town to consult with the committee and describe the way his community faced its similar problem. Nashua's foundation not only filled up "virtually all of the idle Textron property, but also is prepared now to underwrite some $2 million in new buildings." Once upon a time, returning to their agricultural roots would be an alternative for displaced workers, as is often the case for those fallen on in hard times in rural communities, but in Maynard that option was thwarted during World War II, when the federal government took away all the farmland.

And then finally, the official death knell sounded. The *Wall Street Journal* reported that the American Woolen Company was

> *offering its Assabet Mill at Maynard, Mass., for sale or lease through C. W. Whittier and Bros., Boston real estate firm. The mill, formerly the largest woolen mill in the world, has 21 buildings with about one million square feet of floor space. Its operations have been intermittent since the woolen and worsted boom during and just after WWII. The mill has been closed for about six months and its employees notified it will not be reopened.*

Selling the Mill

An aerial view of the mill in 1970, after it had been held for more than fifteen years by Maynard Industries. *Maynard Town Archives*.

The following year, 1953, Maynard Industries, Inc., which consisted of ten Worcester businessmen, bought the mill making it a location for diversified business. One of the first businesses to move in was the Beacon Publishing Company, publisher of several local newspapers, including the *Maynard Beacon-Villager*, in summer of 1953.

Scholars and business management gurus refer to fundamental changes in the organization of a community as restructuring. Modes of restructuring vary widely—for example, there could be changes in the production methods, major changes in the economic basis of a community (such as mill closings), or changes in market mechanisms and local forces. The question is how universal are the problems and the solutions. The factors are numerous and often interrelated. They may stem from international, sectoral, national or local factors. As Finnish researcher Jarmo Kortelainen analyzed it, "in the more diversified communities examined, the need to restructure can be seen as a continuous, if intermittent, evolutionary process, although it can be equally distressing for those affected."

The successful restructuring of the Maynard economy was given quite a bit of airtime in the national press, including the *New York Times*: "Preparing to challenge the notion that the woolen industry must follow the Southern flight of cotton in order to survive...American Woolen Company...has decided to 'go along' with any community that shows an interest in making use of abandoned mill property." Maynard workers were quoted, including fifty-year employee Charley Dyson, who "took the closing of the big Assabet Mill more or less in stride just before Christmas in 1951." The *Times* gave an optimistic assessment of the situation, saying that since Maynard was "a shopping center for an area of 25,000 population, the eventual closing of the mill was only a temporary setback."

The article described the citizens' group, which raised $50,000 in working capital in an effort to attract diversified industry into the one million square feet of available space in twenty-one buildings. It pointed out that while the money was quickly devoured by taxes and reconditioning costs, a guardian angel waited in the wings. Worcester textile executive Louis Pemstein had been watching the possibilities. The article referred back to how the group of businessmen purchased the property from American Woolen Company. Irving Burg became resident manager. "Maynard Industries, Inc., the new operating corporation, reported having rented 52% of the available space. The new industries include plastics, printing, woodworking, warehousing and distributing. With an estimated 200 still unemployed in Maynard, commuting residents are applying for available jobs as each new enterprise takes space."

By 1971 the mill was almost completely filled by the Digital Equipment Corporation (DEC), and the town was once again relying on one major employer. Today, the pendulum has swung back to diversification, with current tenants like Monster.com, Earthwatch, and the Powell Flute Company.

Chapter 11

THE SENSITIVE JUROR
Village Life Contrasted with the Big City

As we have seen in previous chapters, murder was not unheard of in the town of Maynard. In December of 1896, an old farmer on Acton Road, John Deane, was murdered. Deane lived with his three daughters, but all three were in town that day. Lorenzo Barnes, a large man weighing more than 230 pounds was convicted. Barnes had been seen in the area, and was in town later spending money. He bought new boots and threw his old ones in the Assabet River. Police later recovered them from the ice and discovered blood on them. Barnes claimed innocence and said he had happened by Deane's farm while two men were committing the crime and he stopped to try to help Deane. Barnes's death was the last execution by hanging in Massachusetts in the East Cambridge jail on March 4, 1898. There were also the post–World War I gangland murders and other deadly crimes. For the most part, though, Maynard residents lived safely and without fear, but as citizens of the Commonwealth, their civic duty sometimes brought them out into the cruel world that they might otherwise have avoided. Such was the sad story of Willis White.

The *New York Times* described it as the "most brutal crime" committed in Boston in years. Chester Jordan, twenty-nine, a vaudeville actor living at 500 Medford Street in Somerville, confessed to killing his wife, Honora, thirty-seven, in a quarrel on a Tuesday night in early September 1908. To prevent discovery of his crime, Jordan decided to take the body away, stashed in a trunk, on an oceangoing steamer. His plan was to throw the body overboard and then report that his wife had left him. The ship he planned to take was delayed, so Jordan had to hire a cab to take him, with the body in the trunk, to a boardinghouse on Boston's Beacon Hill. The crime was discovered when the cab driver, James Collins, became suspicious and notified police.

A bucolic image representing one side of Maynard's multifaceted character. *Peg Brown.*

A promotional card for Haynes Department Store captures the atmosphere of 1911. *Peg Brown.*

The local distribution of news, good and bad, relied on word of mouth and a variety of printed sources. The Paper Store on Nason Street, shown here, still exists today, albeit in a much changed and diversified form. *Maynard Town Archives*.

Despite having immediately confessed to police upon his arrest, Jordan attempted to avoid a conviction. He disputed the district attorney's ability to prove which of the horrific acts was the actual cause of death. This meant that during the three-week trial, the morbid details were carefully explored, repeatedly. This process must have been unpleasant for all twelve jurors, but it actually drove one of them, Willis A. White, insane. This gave Jordan yet another means to challenge his conviction by calling into question the jury's guilty verdict. If it could be determined that the juror was insane during the trial, no court would hold that it had been a fair trial. What idyllic and peaceful town did the sensitive juror call home? Willis A. White was from Maynard.

During the trial, Jordan's defense team, which was made up of Boston's best criminal defense attorneys, tried to eliminate as causes of death each of his brutal acts: the cutting of the throat, the blows upon the head and the strangulation. Their reasoning was that if the court could not prove beyond a reasonable doubt that any one of those things was the cause of death, then the court would have failed to show that the defendant murdered his wife. Jordan's confession made this ploy useless, but still the court entertained the argument.

Each day the courtroom had been packed with people, many of them women, following every move of the trial. In the district attorney's closing statement, he drew attention to the "hundreds of wives" in Middlesex County who were waiting to hear the verdict. The district attorney's statement was not considered to have been dramatic or emotional, but during the summation, one juror wept openly—Willis White.

White, a cattle driver and horse trader living on Marlboro Road, was a large, robust man, who was known in Maynard for his loud ways. What could bring such a man to the public display of crying?

Ultimately the court instructed the jury that the exact manner in which the defendant killed his wife was immaterial. The jury took their instruction from the court and, after almost eight hours of deliberation, rendered a verdict of guilty of murder in the first degree. For Willis White, however, the damage had been done. Hearing the graphic details of the case and facing the fierce cruelty of the murderer day after day during the trial had been too much.

After the trial, feeling that the mental condition of Willis White was not healthy, White's relatives went before Judge Keyes, at Concord District Court, to make an effort to have White sent to a state institution for treatment. White was brought to Concord in an automobile by his wife, his son Alton and Dr. Frank Rich, Maynard's town physician living on Summer Street. White had been told they were taking him to Cambridge. When the car pulled up in front of the district court building, he began shouting, "I ain't going in there!" He implored the spectators gathered about to "either save him or shoot him."

Several men, including two court officers and Dr. Rich, carried White into the courtroom. There White's behavior was so disruptive that medical personnel had to administer a hypodermic injection to quiet him.

Dr. Rich announced that White's mental faculties, in his opinion, had not been normal for some time, even before he served on the jury. In the court Mrs. White and Dr. Rich filed the necessary application for White to be committed, and with a few other preliminaries and a brief test by Dr. Titcomb and Dr. Rich, the papers were made out. Judge Prescott Keyes, of the district court, decided that White was insane and should be placed under restraint.

General Charles W. Bartlett, counsel for Jordan, learned of the condition of Mr. White and he stated that he would immediately move for a new trial for his client. Two days after White was committed, Chester Jordan's legal team filed a motion for a new trial, on the grounds that White was actually already insane during the trial and when the verdict was rendered.

The other eleven jurors were summoned and testified at a hearing the following September. Among them they were farmers, skilled craftsmen, a bookkeeper, a clerk and a janitor, ranging in age from thirty to sixty-two. Seven of them said they saw nothing during the trial "in the actions, speech, manner or conduct of White different from that of the ordinary, sane, normal man." Four jurors were also cross-examined by the district attorney, testifying that White had not seemed insane until after the verdict. Also testifying was Dr. Quinby, the superintendent of the Worcester Asylum. His opinion was that "White was sane until the day after the verdict, and that his insanity then was due to the reaction from the strain and stress of the trial." Many Maynard residents told a *Boston Globe* reporter that White was just eccentric, a noisy horse trader, but most did not want to go on record with their testimony.

Running counter to this picture, and supporting Jordan's contention, there was testimony to the effect that insanity was hereditary in White's family, along with testimony from neighbors indicating White was insane. Sudbury farmer Arthur A. Dakin testified that in the fifteen years he'd known White, he'd always thought him peculiar because White always "hollered at everyone on the street in driving by, whether he knew them or not." Letters White wrote during the trial were introduced into evidence and these, according to Jordan's defense, suggested White was insane. He had apparently said some odd things to friends and neighbors, claiming to have been drugged while serving on the jury, and that his food had been tampered with.

Weighing all the evidence, the Supreme Judicial Court denied Chester Jordan a new trial. In 1912 Jordan's appeal was heard by the U.S. Supreme Court, where he argued that he had been denied the due process of law by the court in allowing an insane juror to serve on the jury. The court was unanimous in concluding Jordan's claim was without merit, and he was executed in September of that year. Little is known about Willis White's post-trial life, but Jordan's 1911 appeal has been studied since as precedent for cases involving issues of jurors' mental health.

Chapter 12

THE LOST PARATROOPER
Maynard Citizens Afoot in the World

*D*espite being the quiet town that it is, Maynard is not remote and has always been willing to serve up its citizens as actors on a world stage. Sometimes these wanderers found high adventure and good times, such as Betty Marchant, whose travels around the world alone at twenty-seven in the early 1960s, were profiled in the *Washington Post*. After she "shook off the shackles of a stenographer's job at the Massachusetts Institute of Technology," her path led from Maynard to California, Japan, Formosa, Malaya, Indochina, Thailand, Ceylon, India and Jerusalem. Her plan was to get to Zurich, where her skis had been sent from Maynard. Even among other travelers she was set apart by her adventurous attitude, once saying, "Americans abroad mostly live an artificial existence, cut off from the people around them. Their life is too sterile for me."

Others got into trouble of various sorts. The *Chicago Tribune* found Robert McLane, a businessman from Maynard representing a Belgian firm in Europe, when he got mixed up in an "alleged multimillion dollar kickback ring in the army's PX service." McLane testified that at the direction of accused criminals James W. Harlow and Charles E. Wilson, food division purchase chiefs for the army, he deposited $200,000 in a Swiss bank account.

Then there are those from Maynard who served in distant places for the military, and accounts of their lives are not always easy to find. Peg Brown's extensive research uncovered the stories of at least 123 soldiers furnished early on by Assabet Village. In later years, the two World Wars absorbed individuals from Maynard, and after that still more enrolled.

One of Maynard's offerings to the military. *Maynard Town Archives.*

The Lost Paratrooper

Assistant U.S. military attaché Captain Nicholas Rudziak from Maynard was taken into custody on April Fools' Day in 1948 by Polish police, along with his colleague Lieutenant Colonel Frank Jessic, while traveling through Lower Silesia by car. The two men were near a mine, at which the Polish government, with the help of Russian engineers, had been developing what at the time was Europe's second largest deposit of uranium. The police questioned the Americans for several hours before releasing them.

The *New York Times* reported that the U.S. Embassy protested the treatment of the two men as a violation of diplomatic immunity:

> *It is believed they were suspected of having snooped around a uranium mine, although the police charged them with having run over and killed a man with their car. The Americans were released after four hours, only to be stopped at Lodz, where Colonel Jessic's camera and films were confiscated.*
>
> *Polish Foreign Minister Stanislaw Skrzeszewski has handed the U.S. Embassy here a note demanding the immediate annulment of the Mutual Security Act signed by President Truman...The Polish note said many trials in Poland had proved that U.S. diplomatic and consular officials had intervened in Polish affairs. It named...Col. Nicholas Rudziak [and others] as having received intelligence information from alleged terrorist bands and spy rings.*

A person can go all the way from Maynard to Poland's Lower Silesia, but don't try to make a U-turn in the heart of downtown. *Peg Brown.*

Some of Maynard's soldiers ranging far and wide, evinced heroic dimensions. One of these was John Horan, who, after surviving calamity, brought some of the world home with him. The story first surfaced on December 20, 1955, from Ellensburg, Washington. The Associated Press reported that mountaineers had been searching the snow-covered Cascade foothills for a missing army paratrooper named Sergeant John Horan. His Japanese wife and three children had arrived from the Far East expecting him to meet their ship. Horan was twenty-five years old, from Maynard, and he had not been heard from since he had bailed out of a temporarily crippled plane a couple of days previous.

Four days went by with no results until an airline pilot reported the sighting of a fire on a snowy seven-thousand-foot ridge two miles southeast of Mission Peak in the eastern Cascades. This reinvigorated the search. The *Chicago Daily Tribune* reported that soldiers and volunteers would be attempting to reach the area. The fire was considered a significantly hopeful sign, because "normally this time of year there would be no loggers or hunters there, said Ron Lindh, forest ranger."

Just in time for Christmas, the Associated Press reported that the "missing paratrooper who survived a four-day ordeal in a snowbound wilderness hiked out of the mountains to safety at a highway inn west of here today." Horan's stories were frightful. He had to cut his shoes open to relieve his swollen and frostbitten feet. The snow was four or more feet deep. He found a summer mountain cabin where he stayed for two of the days he was missing. He built snowshoes from refrigerator shelves he found in the cabin, and bound them to his numbed feet with strips from his parachute.

"I found a cabin at 8:30 the next morning" after he parachuted, Horan was quoted in the *New York Times*. "It took me twenty-four hours to hike out from it. I kept going all the time. I hiked all night. I can't say how far I hiked. It was very slow because of the deep snow. It was over my head in some places."

Sergeant Horan, on a fifteen-day leave from Fort Bragg, parachuted from the plane, in which he was "hitchhiking" to meet his wife, on orders from the pilot at a time when the plane was out of control. "I didn't know what happened to the plane," Sergeant Horan said to reporters, including one from the *Los Angeles Times*. "I thought I might have been the only survivor…I was following the sounds of trucks and trains and various other sounds I heard down in the valley."

The inn Horan reached was east of the Snoqualmie Pass summit on the main cross-state highway. The newspapers reported that Horan was very concerned about his wife. "Tell her I'm fine," he said. "I'm in very good condition." As the *New York Times* reported it, Sergeant Horan's wife, Teruko, was silent for a moment, then burst into tears of joy when she was notified of her husband's safety. "I am most grateful," she said emotionally, "I am too happy to say more." Her three children were with her when a chaplain broke the news. The search party had been looking for him fifty miles to the northeast of where he was, when they were forced back by a blizzard from the ridge.

Later news reports addressed the questions generated by the story. Why did no one else in the plane jump? Major Glen Pebles, the plane commander, said it was a crowded cockpit and a sticky door. "I was surprised everyone hadn't jumped," Pebles said. "They would all have been gone except for door trouble."

According to Pebles, the plane door would not jettison, and someone had to hold the door open for someone else to jump. When the plane lost power and went into a mild spin over the mountains, Pebles ordered Horan and the other two pilots, Lieutenant R.E. Rigney of San Antonio, Texas, and Lieutenant Richmond Apaka of Lithue, Hawaii, to jump. Pebles said he wasn't wearing his parachute because the small cockpit of the two-engine plane was too crowded for both the chute and his six-foot-four, 220-pound frame. One of the pilots who held the door for Horan came forward to help the major with his parachute.

"Hold it a minute," Pebles said he shouted. "Maybe we're going to pull out O.K."

Pebles did get the plane under control and was able to land safely.

Downtown Maynard as it would have appeared to Teruko Horan, upon arriving from Japan. *Peg Brown.*

Maynard welcomed the Horan family home with open arms. Horan's mother, Mrs. James McGhee, along with a town welcoming committee of fifty people, met Teruko Horan and the three children at the airport. "Upon meeting her daughter-in-law," the *Chicago Tribune* quoted Mrs. McGhee as saying, "I'm quite thrilled, but John wouldn't have married her if she wasn't a wonderful person."

One woman noted with enthusiasm that the sergeant was the first Maynard resident to bring home a Japanese wife. The board of selectmen, with Emile A. Dumas as chairman and head of the welcoming committee, established a fund for a down payment toward the purchase of a new home, and merchants donated Christmas presents to the family.

The story doesn't quite end there. From all readily available information, the duration of the Horans' life in Maynard was blessedly much less eventful than its beginning. They stayed in Maynard, and Teruko worked as an inspector for Digital Equipment Corporation until she retired. In 1990 John and Teruko moved to Florida, where Teruko passed away in 1995. In all, a quietly heroic family it was, and some part of the heroism remains in Maynard. Stories like these, because they really are bigger than the place itself, truly illustrate the spirit of the town.

Chapter 13

MULLIGAN LETTERS AND DUAL MARRIAGES
People Who Hide Out in Maynard

Maynard is far enough from the area's airports and highways that in the early hours of morning, when the trees appear as silhouettes against a sky only beginning to lighten, and the sun is still a distant glow below the horizon, the stillness allows the fleeting impression of being in some remote territory, safely cut off from the cares of the world. Some people run away from here, like John Garlick, a teller at Maynard Trust Company for five years, who disappeared in June 1923, after shorting his accounts $24,000. When Garlick didn't get far, and turned himself in admitting his guilt, the town, in its inimitable fashion, welcomed him home. Two hundred citizens signed a petition to the court asking that he be given probation, not jail time. Signatories included the chief of police, a selectman and bank officers.

In 1902 Robert Fosburgh and his family had hoped to find quiet privacy in their cottage on Brooks Street upon their return to Maynard after Fosburgh was acquitted for the murder of his sister in Pittsfield. While the townspeople filling the streets expressed an intention to honor the family's wishes, the town's enthusiasm in support of Fosburgh could not be contained. The family was first treated to a noisy reception, then a procession of three hundred employees, headed by a platoon of police and a brass band, marched up Main Street to the Fosburgh's house. More than a thousand people had already gathered. There were speeches and cheers.

Others have found that Maynard is an ideal place to hide.

A bookkeeper named Mulligan is one person who retired to Maynard after a life of misadventure and a role in derailing a presidency. Tiny James Mulligan was born in Northern Ireland sometime near 1814. He died in

July of 1894, a resident of Maynard. During those eighty years, he "figured prominently in the political career of James G. Blaine." Mulligan came to the United States when he was fifteen years old, and first worked in a grocery store in Roxbury, now a part of Boston. Mulligan later had his own store on the corner of Prentice and Tremont Streets. In 1851 he became the bookkeeper for a wealthy merchant on North Market Street named Fisher, whose sister James G. Blaine married. The *New York Times* said in Mulligan's obituary that as "the confidential man of this merchant, Mr. Mulligan knew Mr. Blaine intimately."

Blaine was the Republican nominee for president, running against Grover Cleveland. Before the scandal of the Mulligan letters, nothing but rumors marred his chances or stood in his way. Blaine had written the letters to Mr. Fisher, regarding land grant railroad stocks and bonds, and the letters were held with Fisher's consent by Mulligan. In the spring of 1876, strong rumors surfaced regarding Blaine's connection with certain railroad transactions, rumors that were considered serious enough to require Blaine to defend his reputation in a hearing before the House of Representatives.

Blaine faced the specific accusations that he had used his political influence to induce the Atlantic and Pacific Railroad Company; the Missouri, Kansas and Texas Railroad Company; and the Union Pacific Railroad Company to buy from him bonds of the Little Rock and Fort Smith Railroad Company at a price far in excess of their actual value. The letters not only demonstrated these rumors to be true, but also that Blaine had been paid for the bonds several times over.

Blaine's desperation in dealing with the letters is what really sealed his fate. James Mulligan testified in the hearing that not only did Blaine try to get the letters from him, but Blaine also offered Mulligan, a man whose highest position held was that of a bookkeeper, a consulship if he gave the letters back.

As Mulligan testified, "There came a communication from Mr. Blaine, inviting Fisher and me up to his residence." Mulligan did not go, but Fisher did, and relayed the message from Blaine. "Mr. Blaine said that if I should publish them they would ruin him for life, or that if this committee got hold of them they would ruin him for life, and wanted to know if I would not surrender them. I told him 'no.'"

The next evening, Blaine came to Mulligan's hotel, the Riggs House. Blaine and Mulligan met in the lobby, with Blaine asking to at least see the letters and read them. Mulligan refused and retired to his room. Blaine followed him up, and threatened suicide. Mulligan relented and let Blaine read the letters.

The *New York Herald* on June 3, 1876, editorialized, "No one can doubt, after reading the evidence of that curious creature Mulligan, that Mr. Blaine is not worthy of the confidence of the country, and especially in a position as elevated as the Presidency of the United States." The majority of the country agreed, and with the support of Democrats and the Mugwumps—the Republicans disillusioned by Blaine—Grover Cleveland became the twenty-second president in 1885. The "curious creature" Mulligan eventually moved to Maynard, where he lived quietly and anonymously, until his death in 1894.

Josiah Herrick was another curious creature who found Maynard a good place to hide. He figured in the strange story of Mrs. Gertrude Gibbons, alleged husband-poisoner:

Police in Los Angeles were stymied. Deputy District Attorney Keyes had gone ahead and filed a formal charge of murder against Mrs. Gertrude Gibbons for the death by poison of her husband. But the police still had a full investigation ahead of them, because while they were certain of what had happened, they had not found a way to prove it.

Tuberculosis had haunted Frank Gibbons for years. Mrs. Gibbons's story was that she bought the cyanide at Gibbon's own request because he wanted to commit suicide. Los Angeles police detectives did not believe her and thought she had slipped cyanide in place of his medicine. Mrs. Gibbons admitted buying the drug, taking it home, and keeping it in the house overnight. She told of "carefully breaking off a small lump and carefully tying it up in a piece of paper." She said she gave it to her husband just before he went to work Saturday.

In this postcard of Main Street, on the far left is Maynard Trust Company, from which teller John Garlick absconded, leaving his accounts $24,000 short. *Peg Brown.*

A.E. Sathren, assistant superintendent of the Pullman Company, told Detectives Bowe and Taylor that Gibbons arrived at work at the Santa Fe Railroad depot, shortly before noon. He and his coworkers chatted, and Gibbons headed toward his assigned train, where he worked as a conductor. He took a drink of water from the water tap upon entering one of the cars. On his way down the steps of the car, he staggered, clutching his chest, just before he reached the steps of a next car. Mr. Sathren took Gibbons home in a taxicab. Later, at his home at 220 South Bonnie Brae Avenue reported the *Los Angeles Times*, Gibbons expired, shortly after saying, "Well, I'm sorry, but I guess the end has come."

While waiting calmly in her cell at the city jail, Mrs. Gibbons talked freely to reporters, maintaining that she was not guilty. She gave the reporters, including those from the *Los Angeles Times*, the impression of being in complete control of her emotions. "She discusses the past with the same grasp on details as she talks about the present situation and every ramification of the case. 'I have been unhappy in my life with Mr. Gibbons,' she said. 'Constant nagging, continual jealousy all the time.'"

Gertrude Gibbons told the story of her life with Frank Gibbons to the newspapers without any apparent consideration of the consequences. She spoke of there not being much love between them, as if it were quite ordinary. She described how they had known each other for more than ten years, and came to California together. They had gotten married more than four years before. Gibbons was already ill, and as the years went by, his health got worse. With each passing year, as she watched over him and tried to help him, she became more and more resentful. As she put it, in a forthright but quite disturbing way, "since it became apparent he could not recover, he ought to be more careful and thoughtful of others…It was his own idea to commit suicide."

Gertrude Gibbons spun an elaborate context for Frank's supposed suicide. "Time and again after an unusually bad spell he would say it was the only way out of our difficulty," she insisted. The *Los Angeles Times* described Mrs. Gibbons as "a woman of large frame and robust constitution. Her face is somewhat lined, but her carriage and walk, her talk and mannerisms speak of a woman still in the prime of life. Deep chested, well formed, she does not look the 45 years she claims."

The newspapers, particularly the *Los Angeles Times*, promoted the impression that Gertrude Gibbons was living in her own world:

> *I believe in psychology. In spiritual things. From that point of view I do not feel that I have done anything wrong. I am glad his body is liberated, that he's free. We often discussed these things, but he never was positive*

of anything. I think he probably appreciates that I helped him leave his worn-out body and enter the body of a newborn child. You'll understand, that believing as I do, it's hard for me to think that I am looked upon as a murderer.

And what does the story of Mrs. Gibbons have to do with Maynard? A representative of the *Los Angeles Times* found a man named Josiah Herrick, at the Rich Farm in Maynard. Herrick was Gertrude Gibbons's first husband, from whom she had never been divorced. When contacted by the press, Herrick said he and Gertrude had gotten married twenty years before in Boston. They had met when she was bookkeeper for W.D. Brown and Company dry goods in Gloucester, and her name before their marriage was Gertrude Stewart. They first lived in Gloucester for several years and then moved to Cambridge. Their relationship ran into some difficulty, and ultimately they agreed to separate. Gertrude went to East Boston to live with her sister and help her run a lodging house in the Central Square section. Frank Gibbons was at that time living in East Boston and was known as the Beau Brummel of Noddle's Island, probably because of his fashion sense and dandyism. He was said to frequent the Stewart sisters' lodging house, where he likely met Gertrude. Josiah and Gertrude occasionally exchanged letters, but they never again lived together after their separation. They never got a divorce. When he was told of Gertrude's marriage to another man and her subsequent alleged murder of that second husband, Herrick did not seem affected by the news.

The newspapers loved this development. "If Mrs. Gertrude Gibbons is cleared on the charge of having murdered her second husband, Frank C. Gibbons…she may have to face a bigamy charge," reported the *Los Angeles Times*. "Mrs. Gibbons admits that she went through a marriage ceremony with Gibbons here without having divorced her first husband, Josiah Herrick."

On December 25, 1918, the newspapers reported that Dr. Lyman B. Stookey and Professor Arthur R. Maas, who did the second chemical analysis of the organs and blood of Frank Gibbons, had found significant amounts of cyanide present, seemingly almost like a Christmas gift to the authorities. This news was short-lived, however, as subsequent article reported just the opposite. Eventually it became clear that the experts were sharply divided into two camps—Stookey, District Attorney Thomas Lee Woolwine and Professor Robert E. Swain signed off on reports finding cyanide in the body, while Coroner Hartwell, Autopsy Surgeon Wagner, Maas, Professor Laird J. Stabler and City Chemist Erwin H. Miller declared Gibbons's death was due to natural causes, with no trace of cyanide found.

What accused murderer wouldn't want the town to bring out the band and have a parade upon their return from trial? In this image, the occasion is the fiftieth anniversary of the town in 1921. *Maynard Town Archives*.

The *Los Angeles Times* also reported that Maynard resident Josiah Herrick had decided not to press bigamy charges against Gertrude Gibbons. In fact, according to the newspaper, Herrick continued to seem completely unperturbed at the thought that his former wife was accused of murder and didn't even seem to accept the reports that she had married someone else. He'd "received no official" word of it. He certainly had no intention of going to California to appear in court. In the *Los Angeles Times*, Gertrude put it this way: "I knew he would not do anything to harm me. You know, I feel that if he were here he'd stick by me and help me in every way."

Ultimately, the grand jury hearing the case decided against indicting Gertrude Gibbons. Nearly twenty-five witnesses testified before the grand jury, and many spoke favorably of Mrs. Gibbons. After debating for under a half hour, the jurors, among them four women, announced the refusal to indict. Upon her release from the county jail, where she had been for almost a month, Gertrude Gibbons had plenty to say to reporters. She claimed to be a changed woman, but didn't say in what way. She did say that she'd been studying philosophy during her incarceration and was planning to teach people to be happy. The insurance money that she had been awarded for her husband's death would enable her to go into this work. Finally, she announced her intention to go somewhere where no one knows her and try to be forgotten.

Maybe Gertrude decided to drop in on Josiah Herrick, and maybe she, too, ended up hiding out in Maynard.

Chapter 14

WORLD WAR II AND THE GOVERNMENT TAKEOVER

*D*uring World War II, some of the town was lost to the federal government, never to be returned as private property. In 2005 the government gave the land back to the public as the Assabet River National Wildlife Refuge. Walking there now, the remaining old roads and housing foundations are interrupted by the toxic noise of war, in the form of ordnance storage sheds, ammunition dumps and the like. Who lived here in this lost part of Maynard? Where did those former residents go?

Peg Brown, a local history buff and raconteur, tells of one man who returned to his former home for the first time only a couple years ago. The area was not yet open to the public because of lingering safety hazards and toxic waste, but a group of interested citizens led by a government official toured the site. The man saw his old yard, and approached the front steps, all that remained of his house, and collapsed in tears. As Peg describes it, "When it was time to leave, for the longest time we couldn't get him to come along, until finally we did. It was heartbreaking."

It was April of 1942 when more than one hundred individual property owners in the towns of Maynard, Hudson, Stow and Sudbury, agreed to sell a total of 3,100 acres of land to the federal government. The government also needed an ammunition depot. These 800 acres of Maynard's valuable farm and residential land included the Henry Ford farm (once known as Gately's farm), the Puffer homesteads, Don Lent's family home, the Jim Haynes farm belonging to the Sarvela family and Puffers Pond. The Vose Farm, formerly the Rice Tavern, went as well with Vose Pond, which had been used by the local Finnish people as a summer resort. Some of these farms and estates were built in the 1700s, and many of the landowners had lived there for several generations. The area Maynard lost was considered by many to be its most valuable and picturesque. The military named the area the Maynard Ordnance Supply Depot, and any roads entering the area were closed off, including Puffer Road, Old Marlboro Road, Taylor Road, White Pond Road and Craven Road.

A few years later, in 1955, the *New York Times* reported the announcement by the Universal Match Corporation that they were taking over the operation of the Maynard Ordnance Test Station from the Army Ordnance Corps. The match company planned to use the station to perform "research and development work on a wide variety of ordnance items," with actual operations beginning in the new fiscal year. Universal Match Corporation was not only a leading manufacturer of advertising matchbooks, but also held defense contracts for making flares, firing devices and other products at the Longhorn Ordnance Works in Marshall, Texas.

Virtually all of the land used for agriculture within the boundaries of Maynard were included in the eight hundred acres sold to the government. *Maynard Town Archives.*

On much of the farmland stood houses such as this one, but the area is now thoroughly wooded, returned to its precultivated state, having been overtaken by trees. *Maynard Town Archives*.

As the years went by, the area became known officially as the U.S. Army's Fort Devens Sudbury Training Annex, covering 2,230 acres, about 3.5 square miles. At some point the land became more of a financial drain and management headache than an asset, so the machinery went into gear to jettison it. Interested takers included the U.S. Fish and Wildlife Service for 2,205 acres, the U.S. Air Force for another 4.1 acres and the Federal Emergency Management Agency for 71.4 acres.

Before opening to the public, the land had to be decontaminated from the military's use. The Center for Disease Control (CDC) did a detailed assessment of the toxicity situation. Railroad yards, bunkers and test areas radiated with residue from explosives and from spilled chemicals. A leach field stood loaded with septic waste. Puffer Pond hosted what the CDC called "spoils" and chemicals. Various buildings still had remains of fuels, pesticide, heating oil and drums containing unknown substances. Abandoned buildings and bunkers stood scattered throughout.

Government activity in the area had positive effects on Maynard's economy. The Maynard Motel would likely have hosted many a military-affiliated guest. *Peg Brown.*

Natick Army Research and Development Command had converted one bungalow into an animal-testing lab in the 1960s. The bungalow was also used as a guesthouse, and at one point the heating oil storage tank in the basement overflowed and residue remained.

Between 1965 and 1972, a testing program operated, in which clothing was soaked with fifty-seven grams of mustard gas to measure its absorptive properties. Twenty-four trash bags of the cloth, treated with bleach, were buried, along with contaminated combat gear.

Trespassers, unknowingly or carelessly, dumped trash, rode dirt bikes and shot target practice in various places throughout the area. Polychlorinated biphenyls (PCBs), toxic substances known to cause cancer and other ill effects, waited for anyone foolish enough to scavenge parts or vandalize transformers in a certain spill area. The toxins impacted watersheds on all sides of the military annex, particularly the Assabet River, White Pond and private wells on Old Puffer Road, Parker Street and Riverside Park.

Cleanup activities began in 1985, and in the course of it the army removed more than 15,000 cubic yards of contaminated soil and more than three hundred tanks and drums. They also capped the Old Gravel Pit landfill, which covered about two acres.

In the spring of 2002, the Environmental Protection Agency officially removed the area from its list of Superfund sites, which freed the property for reuse. Wooded with white pine and mixed hardwoods, some of the area is wetlands, including a white cedar swamp and an assortment of bogs and vernal pools. The Assabet River Wildlife Refuge opened to the public in March of 2005, with ten miles of trails and no dogs allowed.

Chapter 15

COLLISIONS AT THE
RAIL CORRIDOR
Maynard, Old and New

The rail corridor formerly used by the Boston and Maine Railroad runs right through the middle of Maynard, and is now in the process of becoming the Assabet River Rail Trail. Collisions at points along the tracks have occurred throughout the years, and they still occur, but in a different way. Some of the collisions are remembered, others forgotten; some publicized, others known only to the people concerned.

On a November night in 1905, a Boston and Maine local train left the city, bound on the Fitchburg line for Maynard and other towns in the valley of the Assabet River. By the time the four full cars had progressed to Baker's Bridge, heavy traffic had made the train late. Fog in the valley obscured visibility, so the Montreal Express train, traveling thirty-five miles per hour did even slow down before it crashed into the rear of the local train. Eighteen people died and twenty-five were seriously injured.

The *Boston Globe* called it "Maynard's Day of Sorrow," with at least seven of the dead from Maynard: May Campbell, vice president of the ladies auxiliary of the local Hibernian lodge; William J. Barris and his three-year-old son, Irving; Mr. and Mrs. Andrew Carlson; George Czujko; and Vladislav Matiulievicz. Alfreda Batley was on the "dangerous list" for days, with internal injuries and a crushed leg. Her husband Albert E. Batley, was also hospitalized, with a broken leg and head injury.

In 1911 a train derailed adjacent to the American Woolen Company siding, at Lawton's Crossing near the Maynard station, injuring five. The injured were taken in and cared for in the homes of neighboring residents Mrs. James Prosper and Ellen Sullivan. Often the siding would have cars standing for loading of goods from the mill, but this particular day the siding was clear.

The streetside view of the Boston and Maine Railroad Station in 1912, not long after the 1911 calamity. *Maynard Town Archives.*

Wreckage from the 1905 collision of a Boston and Maine train with a Montreal express that left at least eighteen people dead from the impact or from the fire that followed. *Maynard Town Archives.*

Mrs. Albert Batley, a survivor of the 1905 calamity. *Maynard Town Archives.*

Any commotion, happy or tragic, brought Maynard's residents out full force. *Maynard Town Archives.*

This image captures the mixed blessing of the rail service, in its romantic snow- and smoke-filled depiction of the exact spot where many of the car-train collisions occurred. *Maynard Town Archives.*

One December evening in 1923, shortly after eight o'clock, William Creeley drove his Ford out of Nason Street into Summer Street. Even then, the road climbed uphill from Nason Street to the railroad crossing, and Creeley had driven it many times. This time, Creeley traveled up Summer Street and stopped at the flagman's shanty. He looked both up the track toward Acton and back. He could see past the "granary," about four or five hundred feet. He listened, heard no signal, "saw that the track was clear" and began to go over the crossing. His car was struck on the right side, in the rear, by a Boston and Maine engine.

According to Creeley, while he knew there was a train due to come into Maynard from Boston around 7:30 p.m., he did not know that train was late. In addition, the engineer failed to give a signal, the train was speeding and there was no flagman giving warning of approaching trains. In the original trial, Creeley was awarded $7,000. The railroad appealed, however, and the court ruled in favor of Boston and Maine, judging that Creeley was guilty of "contributory negligence."

Another collision occurred in February of 1951. Ernest Ladd, his wife and two friends left the Ladd's home in Waltham in the evening to go to a restaurant in Maynard. Just as they were settling in, heavy snow began falling, so they decided to head back immediately. At a crossing in Sudbury about midnight, their car struck the center of a freight train. This was an open country crossing, and aside from the heavy snowfall and the lack of streetlights in the vicinity, there was nothing that would have obstructed their view of the train. Perhaps because the headlights of the car were at a downward slant and showed only about three feet above the ground, no one in the automobile saw the freight train until it appeared directly in front of them. Ladd was unable to stop the car and, caught by the middle car of the long freight train, it was dragged for fifty feet. Mrs. Ladd was thrown from the car. Once the automobile became freed from the train, Ladd used the red lights on the rear of the caboose of the freight train to search for his wife. When Ernest Ladd sued the train company for damages, the train company won on appeal. The court pronounced that it was "hard to see why the passengers in the automobile did not hear the train." Again the railroad was saved by the concept of contributory negligence.

Now that the trains are gone, what kind of collisions could there be? Rather than collisions of vehicles, there are collisions of values, and of ideas about how the rail corridor should, and should not, be used. As the town changes, people stay or go. While its personality is always unique, many aspects of Maynard are not static. Why did the Finns leave Maynard, for example? The homes near the mill and where the old train station stood have for whatever reason always housed the people with the least financial agility.

Maynard's old high school building now houses Artspace, a vibrant collection of artists' studios, and Acme Theater Productions.

In the late 1960s and early 1970s, there were new arrivals from Puerto Rico who settled here. Finnish children were warned away from this neighborhood, and shortly thereafter there was a Finnish exodus, Maynard's version of "white flight." One family left, for example, the patriarch of which had been a founder of the United Cooperative Society. He and his wife retired and moved to Florida, while their children and grandchildren moved just a little farther west in Massachusetts, near where other Finns had moved. Changes in the town continue.

On a recent sunny Tuesday, there appeared on the Assabet River Rail Trail two white plastic trash bags, full of Bud Light cans, cartons and other party refuse. Someone had tossed them onto the trail from the street above. It would seem that at least one Maynard resident prefers to dump trash illegally, rather than buy the sticker required to have it picked up from the curb. By the next day, the Bud Light cans had been removed from the bags. Someone industrious would be turning in the cans for a deposit refund. If the owner of the trash had done this, there might have been enough money to buy a sticker for the bag. If the recyclables, which are picked up curbside for free, had been removed from the bags as well, there would have been no need to cart the trash to the other side of town to dump it. Residents of a house adjacent to the Rail Trail picked up the trash, put a sticker on the bag and put it out at their own curb. This was a collision between differing views on respect for the land.

So, conflicts among humans continue to find expression along the rail corridor. Collisions involving vehicles have become collisions of aesthetics. Certainly life and limb are no longer in danger, but now it's the quality of the life and the fitness of limb that are at issue. As more people understand what the rail corridor can be, perhaps the collisions will fade into the past.

Epilogue

MAYNARD, QUINTESSENTIAL AND UNIQUE

Never just an ordinary mill town, Maynard sits in the sights of the pundits, the social analysts, the commercial and business administrators, even the federal government. Business experts and economists have long looked to Maynard as an exemplar of all aspects of the mill town economy. Socialism had its heyday, with the Finnish and British cooperatives, prosperous and flourishing throughout the twentieth century and studied by esteemed economists.

There was a flurry of national attention when the American Woolen Company first closed in 1950. The nation watched as the company attempted to justify its decision, while the town rallied a committee to take some kind of remedial action. A front-page story in the business section of the *New York Times* in 1954 described the successful efforts of a citizen's group to raise the money needed to entice diversified industry into the mill property.

In 1993 Maynard once again had the attention of national business interests as they watched to see what would happen when the Digital Equipment Corporation left the scene, "abandoning the red brick mill complex," as the *Wall Street Journal* colorfully put it. The *New York Times* analyzed the rebound in 2003, saying that it was possible to "take the pulse of the American economy" by Maynard, and that "the ups and downs here over the course of 150 years" are a microcosm of "the country's financial health."

More than just of interest to the wider world, Maynard has been a special place for people to live and grow up. In his collection of poems entitled *Pieces,* Robert Creeley, a former New York State Poet Laureate, has remembered his West Acton boyhood as

Epilogue

*Smell of gum wrappers as of Saturday afternoon at movies
in Maynard, Mass.—*

In 1902, the *Boston Daily Globe* did a lengthy puff piece describing the American Woolen Company's huge and positive impact on the town since the addition of the Assabet Mill to A.M.C. holdings in 1899. The article called Maynard "an ideal manufacturing community...touched with a magic hand."

So, Maynard continues as a quintessential mill town with no mill, while at the same time its unique qualities endure and distinguish it from other towns in the area. Where else do Bolsheviks and Wobblies, the religious and the atheists, the law-abiding citizens, the rogues and the scalawags live peaceably, side by side? Where else has an entire town been sued for libel? Where else do people go to court to fight over who has the right to divert the river? With Mafia murders, bank teller thievery, a lost paratrooper, family tragedies and Mulligan letters, Maynard has seen its share of drama, political intrigue and comedy. How does such a diverse and contentious citizenry live so harmoniously? In the words of a local businesswoman, it's just "magical Maynard."

Here the George F. Brown House, built around 1830 and surrounded in this photograph by the cultural detritus of all the subsequent years, reveals many of the collisions of time found throughout the story of Maynard, Massachusetts. *Maynard Town Archives.*

BIBLIOGRAPHY

BOOKS AND ARTICLES

Aaltonen, Frank. *Maynard Weavers: The Story of the United Co-operative Society of Maynard.* Maynard: United Co-operative Society, 1941.

Blaine, James Gillespie. *The Mulligan Letters: How Speaker Blaine Prostituted His High Office for Personal Gain.* N.p., 1884.

Boothroyd, Paul, and Lewis Halprin. *Maynard, Massachusetts: Images of America.* Mount Pleasant, SC: Arcadia Publishing, 1999.

Brown, Peggy Jo. *Hometown Soldiers: Civil War Veterans of Assabet Village and Maynard, Massachusetts.* Maynard: Flying Heron Press, 2005.

Cameron, Ardis. *Radicals of the Worst Sort: Laboring Women in Lawrence, Massachusetts, 1860–1912.* Urbana: University of Illinois Press, 1993.

Creeley, Robert. "Smell of gum wrappers." *Pieces.* New York: Charles Scribner's Sons, 1969.

Garber, Marjorie. *Sex and Real Estate: Why We Love Houses.* New York: Pantheon Books, 2000.

Garrelick, Renee. *Clothier of the Assabet: The Mill and Town of Edward Carver Damon.* Concord: R. Garrelick, 1988.

Gutteridge, William H. *A Brief History of the Town of Maynard, Massachusetts.* Town of Maynard, 1921.

Hart, John F. "Property Rights, Costs, and Welfare: Delaware Water Mill Legislation, 1719–1859." *Journal of Legal Studies* 27, no.2 (June 1998): 455–71.

Herring, Harriet L. *Passing of the Mill Village: Revolution in a Southern Institution.* Chapel Hill: University of North Carolina Press, 1949.

Hoglund, A. William. "Breaking with Religious Tradition: Finnish Immigrant Workers and the Church, 1890–1915." In Passi, *For the Common Good*, 23–64.

———. *Finnish Immigrants in America, 1880–1920.* Madison: University of Wisconsin Press, 1960.

Bibliography

Hummasti, P. George. "'The Workingman's Daily Bread': Finnish American Working Class Newspapers, 1900–1921." In Passi, *For the Common Good*, 167–94.

Jokinen, Walfrid John. "Economic Activities of the Finns in the United States." In *Old Friends , Strong Ties*, edited by Vilho Niitema, et al, 103–14. Turku: Institute for Migration, 1978.

Jura, Art. *Fenni—The Finns Among Us: A History of the Finns in New England and Beyond*. Rockport, ME: Picton Press, 2001.

Kero, Reino. "The Background of Finnish Immigration." In *The Finns in North America: A Social Symposium*. Ralph J. Jalkanen, ed., 55–62. Hancock, MI: Suomi College, 1969.

———. "Finnish Immigrant Culture in America." In *Old Friends – Strong Ties*, Vilho Niitema, et al, eds., 115–43. Turku: Institute for Migration, 1976.

Kortelainen, Jarmo. "Mill Closure—Options for a Restart: A Case-study of Local Response in a Finnish Mill Community" in *Local Economic Development: A Geographical Comparison of Rural Community Restructuring*. Cecily Neil and Markku Tykkylainen, eds. United Nations University Press

Kostiainen, Auvo. "For or Against Americanization? The Case of the Finnish Immigrant Radicals." In *American Labor and Immigration History, 1877–1920s*, edited by Dirk Hoerder, 259–275. Urbana: University of Illinois Press, 1983.

———. "The Tragic Crisis: Finnish-American Workers and the Civil War in Finland." In Passi, *For the Common Good: Finnish Immigrants and the Radical Response to Industrial America*, 217–35.

Kulik, Gary, et al., eds. *The New England Mill Village, 1790–1860*. Cambridge: MIT Press, 1982.

Ladenheim, Melissa. *The Sauna in Central New York*. Ithaca: Dewitt Historical Society of Tompkins County, 1986.

Ledy, Nancy B., and Ellen Lefkowitz, Note, *Judgment By Your Peers? The Impeachment of Jury Verdicts and the Case of the Insane Juror*, 21 N.Y.L.F. 57, 83 (1975).

Mather, Cotton, and Matti Kaups. "The Finnish Sauna: A Cultural Index to Settlement." *Annals of the Association of American Geographers*, 53, no. 4 (Dec 1963) 494–504.

The Mulligan Letters: A Complete Edition, Comprising All the Letters Arranged in Order of Their Dates. N.p., 1884?

Passi, Michael M., ed. *For the Common Good: Finnish Immigrants and the Radical Response to Industrial America*. Superior, WI: Tyomies Society, 1977.

Reppetto, Thomas. *American Mafia: A History of Its Rise to Power*. New York: Henry Holt and Company, 2004.

Roddy, Edward G. *Mills, Mansions, and Mergers: The Life of William M. Wood*. North Andover: Merrimack Valley Textile Museum, 1982.

Rogers, Alan. "Murder in Massachusetts: The Criminal Discovery Rule from Snelling to Rule 14." *American Journal of Legal History.* 40, no. 4 (October 1996): 438–54. JSTOR.

Ross, Carl. *The Finn Factor in American Labor, Culture, and Society*. New York Mills, MN: Part Printers, Inc., 1977.

Sheridan, Ralph L., et al. *History of Maynard, Massachusetts, 1871–1971*. Town of Maynard Historical Committee, 1971.

BIBLIOGRAPHY

Sommer, Robin Langley. *The American House*. San Diego: Thunder Bay Press, 2000.

Teass, Horace A. "Water and Water Courses: Riparian Rights." *Virginia Law Review*, 18, no. 3 (Jan 1932) 223–48.

Turner, Howard Haines. *Case Studies of Consumers' Cooperatives*. New York: Columbia University Press, 1941.

Wargelin, John. *The Americanization of the Finns*. Hancock, MI: The Finnish Lutheran Book Concern, 1924.

Watson, Bruce. *Bread and Roses: Mill, Migrants, and the Struggle for the American Dream*. New York: Viking, 2005.

WEBSITES

Aaland, Mikkel. "History of the Nordic Bath." *Finnish Sauna*. http://www.cyberbohemia.com/Pages/saunaamerica.htm.

"Assabet River National Wildlife Refuge." *U.S. Fish and Wildlife Service*. http://www.fws.gov/refuges/profiles

"Environmental Update: New England Army Installation Deleted from EPA Superfund National Priorities List." *U.S. Army Environmental Center*. http://aec.army.mil/usaec/publicaffairs/update

Raivaaja. http://www.raivaaja.org

COURT CASES AND OTHER GOVERNMENT DOCUMENTS

All cases were provided full-text by LexisNexis.

Arthur H. Howland v. Inhabitants of Maynard. Supreme Judicial Court of Massachusetts. 159 Mass. 434; 34 N.E. 515; 1893 Mass. LEXIS 177. June 1, 1893, Argued; June 2, 1893, Argued; July 14, 1893, Decided.

Benjamin W. Gleason & another vs. Assabet Manufacturing Company. Supreme Judicial Court of Massachusetts. 101 Mass. 72; 1869 Mass. LEXIS 141. January, 1869, Decided.

Charles H. Cheney & others v. Bartholomew J. Coughlin & another. Supreme Judicial Court of Massachusetts, Middlesex, 201 Mass. 204; 87 N.E. 744; 1909 Mass. LEXIS 705 December 2, 1908, February 26, 1909.

Commonwealth v. Chester S. Jordan. Supreme Judicial Court of Massachusetts, Middlesex, 207 Mass. 259; 93 N.E. 809; 1911 Mass. LEXIS 677 November 17, 1910; November 18, 1910; January 3, 1911.

Ernest H. Ladd & others v. The New York, New Haven and Hartford Railroad Company. Supreme Judicial Court of Massachusetts. 335 Mass. 117; 138 N.E.2d 346; 1956 Mass. LEXIS 585. October 4, 1956, Argued. December 4, 1956, Decided.

(House No. 2100, 1938), pursuant to Chapter 32, Resolves of 1937, Mass. Acts and Resolves, 1937.

Nora M. Splaine v. American Powder Company, Supreme Judicial Court of Massachusetts, 298 Mass. 114; 10 N.E.2d 87; 1937 Mass. LEXIS 863, October 8, 1936, Argued, September 15, 1937, Decided.

Sheehan v. Goriansky, Supreme Judicial Court of Massachusetts, 317 Mass. 10; 56 N.E.2d 883; 1944 Mass. LEXIS 791. *Sheehan v. Goriansky, Supreme Judicial Court of Massachusetts*, 321 Mass. 200; 72 N.E.2d 538; 1947 Mass. LEXIS 615.

Stasiukevich v. Nicolls. 168 F. (2d) 474. U.S. Circuit Ct. App., First Circuit, May 27, 1948. 1948 U.S. App. LEXIS 2069.

Thomas E. King v. American Powder Company. Supreme Judicial Court of Massachusetts, 290 Mass. 464; 195 N.E. 785; 1935 Mass. LEXIS 1354, April 1, 1935, Argued; April 29, 1935, Decided.

William A. Creeley v. Boston and Maine Railroad. Supreme Judicial Court of Massachusetts. 263 Mass. 529; 161 N.E. 584; 1928 Mass. LEXIS 1170. March 29, 1928, Argued. May 25, 1928, Decided.

NEWSPAPERS

All newspaper articles were provided full-text by Proquest Historical Newspapers, except the Maynard newspapers on microfilm at the Maynard Public Library.

"18 Dead, 45 Hurt in Boston Wreck." *Chicago Daily*, November 27, 1905.

"Actor Killed Wife and Cut Up Body." *New York Times*, September 4, 1908.

"Agitators Busy in Maynard." *Maynard Enterprise*, April 23, 1919.

"Air Snapped and Earth Shook." *Boston Daily Globe*, March 5, 1889.

"Alleged Borgia Plot Spreads." *Los Angeles Times*, December 19, 1918.

"American Woolen Co.: Assabet Mills will Suspend Operations When Present Orders are Run Out." *Wall Street Journal*, November 8, 1930.

"American Woolen Co." *Wall Street Journal*, November 12, 1907.

"American Woolen Puts a New England Mill Up for Sale of Lease." *Wall Street Journal*, June 27, 1952.

"Body Hacked: Maynard Man Believed Murdered Found in Charles River." *Maynard [Enterprise]*, 20:46, Friday, 28 [or 23] March 1919.

"Closed Mill Stirs Town into Action." *New York Times*, November 5, 1950.

"Crazy Man on Jury that Convicted Jordan." *Atlanta Constitution*, May 9, 1909.

"Cyanide Found in Body." *Los Angeles Times*, December 25, 1918.

"Dies in Tank of Boiling Water." *Boston Daily Globe*, July 7, 1916.

"Dual Marriage Proven." *Los Angeles Times*, December 22, 1918.

"Dynamite Factory Blows Up; F.B.I. Seeks Clues of Sabotage." *Los Angeles Times*, January 18, 1940.

"Experts Find Cyanide." *Los Angeles Times*, December 28, 1918.

Fenton, John H. "Towns Challenge Closing of Mills," *New York Times*, April 4, 1954.

"Fire Sighted on Peak; Seek Lost 'Chutist" *Chicago Daily Tribune*, December 22, 1955.

"Five Injured, 60 Shaken Up." *Boston Daily Globe*, April 17, 1911.

"Flier Lost as Family Arrives." *New York Times*, December 21, 1955.

"Here is Why Paratrooper Chuted Alone." *Chicago Daily Tribune*, December 28, 1955.

"Italy Not Responsible." *New York Times*, March 15, 1909.

"James Mulligan is Dead." *New York Times*, July 29, 1894.

BIBLIOGRAPHY

"Japanese Wife Arrives to Find GI Lost." *Los Angeles Times*, December 21, 1955.

"May Ask for Continuance." *Los Angeles Times*, December 26, 1918.

Maynard Enterprise, August 28, 1940.

"Mother Meets Japanese Wife of GI Air Survivor." *Chicago Daily Tribune*, December 26, 1955.

"Mrs. Gibbons Free Today." *Los Angeles Times*, January 17,1919.

"Ordnance Test Deal Set." *New York Times*, April 24, 1955.

"Poles Develop Uranium Mine in Deep Secrecy: American Expelled for Too Close a Look." *Chicago Daily Tribune*. April 12, 1948.

"Polish Note Demands U.S. End 'Intervening.'" *Washington Post*, December 3, 1951.

"Prominent Saloonmen." *National Police Gazette*, September 28, 1901.

"Robert S. Fosburgh is Placed on Trial." *New York Times*, July 19, 1902.

"Seized for Murder Kneeling at Grave: Tenafly Man, Hunted Six Years, is recognized at Father-in-Law's Funeral." *New York Times*, August 23, 1925.

"Soldier Survives Four-Day Ordeal." *New York Times*, December 23, 1955.

"Spinners Go Out on Strike." *Atlanta Constitution*, January 16, 1902.

"Taking the World in Stride." *Washington Post*, June 10, 1962.

"The Famous 'Mulligan Letters'." *New York Times*, July 20, 1894.

"To Face Bigamy Charge?" *Los Angeles Times*, December 23, 1918.

"U.S. Charges Poles Held 2 Aides From Embassy." *New York Times*, April 9, 1948.

"U.S. Food Buyer Disowns Army Kickback Ring." *Chicago Daily Tribune*, October 1, 1953.

"Welcomed by Employees." *Boston Daily Globe*, July 28, 1901.

Visit us at
www.historypress.net